ECONOMIC DEVELOPMENT 101

THE BASICS FOR

Board Members, Committee Chairs

and Other Volunteer Leaders

By
David L. Goetsch

ABOUT THE AUTHOR

Dr. Goetsch is Vice-President of Okaloosa-Walton College in Okaloosa County, Florida where his responsibilities include, among other things, business, industry, local government, and military relations as well as economic development. Having authored more than 60 books in the fields of business, management, leadership, and economic development, he is one of the most widely published college professors in the United States. Four of Dr. Goetsch's books are best-sellers and three have been translated into foreign languages (Korean, Indonesian, and Malaysian).

Dr. Goetsch is co-founder, past-president, and policy board member of the Okaloosa Economic Development Council, board member of the Walton Economic Development Council, two time past president and current foundation board member of the Niceville-Valparaiso Chamber of Commerce, past president and current board member of the Fort Walton Beach Chamber of Commerce, past board member of the Crestview Chamber of Commerce, past foundation board member of the Walton County chamber of Commerce, founder of the Technology Coast Manufacturing & Engineering Network (TeCMEN), and co-founder and past board chair of the Gulf Coast Alliance for Technology Transfer (GCATT). Dr. Goetsch was the Florida Economic Development Council's Economic Development Volunteer of the Year in 1992 and 1996 for northwest Florida.

CONTACTING THE AUTHOR

Dr. Goetsch welcomes questions, feedback, and comments from readers. He may be contacted at the following email address:

ddsg2001@cox.net

CONTENTS

■

■

■

Introduction

■■
■■

CIVIC ENTREPRENEURSHIP AND THE VOLUNTEER LEADER

The term "entrepreneurship" is typically associated with innovative, visionary people who turn ideas into businesses. An entrepreneur, in the traditional sense, sees a need, finds an innovative way to meet that need, and takes the risks necessary to turn the innovation into a product or service providing business. Entrepreneurs create businesses that, in turn, create jobs. Characteristics associated with entrepreneurs include vision, internal-motivation, a positive attitude, unconventional thinking, persuasiveness, leadership, perseverance, and the ability to build consensus between individuals and groups that have differing and sometimes conflicting agendas.

Civic entrepreneurship involves applying these same characteristics to the economic development of local communities and regions. Civic entrepreneurs are community leaders who have a vision for their community and who pursue that vision with creativity, innovation, and all of the other characteristics associated with business entrepreneurs. Community leaders who serve as volunteer leaders of local economic development councils (EDOs) are civic entrepreneurs. If you are reading this book as part of your service in a local EDO, you are a civic entrepreneur.

As a volunteer leader and civic entrepreneur you will be called upon to apply all of the characteristics associated with entrepreneurs as you attempt to: 1) bring various individuals and groups to the table and persuade them to put aside their personal agendas for the greater good of the community; 2) persuade local elected officials to support the EDO's vision for economic development; 3) lead teams of volunteers in planning and implementing economic development projects; and 4) persevere through controversy, apathy, resistance, insufficient resources, and other obstacles that stand in the way of the economic development of the community.

EXAMPLES OF CIVIC ENTREPRENEURSHIP

Business entrepreneurs start companies of their own, but civic entrepreneurs encourage and facilitate the start-up of companies for other people. Consequently, business entrepreneurs and civic entrepreneurs are natural allies. The remaining chapters in this book explain what civic entrepreneurs need to know in order to be catalysts for economic development in their communities. The examples of civic entrepreneurship that follow are provided to illustrate the concept in practical terms that will make it easier to understand.

Business Entrepreneur Becomes a Civic Entrepreneur

Mack Pelham is a business entrepreneur who became a civic entrepreneur. He used to be a real estate property manager. Now Pelham owns a small business that provides hurricane protection for residential dwellings located on Florida's Gulf Coast. In the old days, every time a hurricane entered the Gulf of Mexico, Pelham would receive frantic calls from the out-of-state owners of the condominiums he managed. With every call, Pelham would be forced to rush around to hardware stores hoping to purchase enough of a rapidly dwindling supply of plywood to board up the windows of his client's condominiums.

After a particularly active hurricane season, an exhausted and exasperated Pelham thought, "There must be a better way." While researching the various approaches to hurricane protection, Pelham came across several different versions of a window covering system that, once installed, could be easily rolled down whenever a hurricane threatened. He began contacting his owners and encouraging them to install the roll-down hurricane shutters. Most of the owners liked the idea, but there was a problem. Pelham could find no one to install the shutters.

Out of frustration, Pelham learned how to install the shutter systems himself. As often happens, one thing led to another and before long Pelham had developed a successful hurricane protection business on the side. After a couple of years, he left his job in property management and turned his part-time side job into a full-time business. The decision paid off. Pelham now franchises this business in 12 different cities with new franchises being added regularly.

Pelham is now a successful business entrepreneur, but the transition from employee to employer was not easy for him. He learned a lot in the process; most of it the hard way. Knowing that other budding entrepreneurs probably experience similar difficulties in trying to start new businesses, Pelham decided he wanted to help. He now shares what he has learned by chairing the Small Business Start-Up Committee of his local EDO; a committee he founded.

Pelham has become an invaluable member of his EDO, a board member whose help is frequently sought by others who have ideas they would like to turn into businesses. By founding his EDO's Small Business Start-Up Committee and chairing it, Pelham has become more than just a business entrepreneur—he is also a civic entrepreneur.

College President and Civic Entrepreneur

Dr. James R. "Bob" Richburg, President of Okaloosa-Walton College in northwest Florida, already had a long record of civic entrepreneurship when he helped found the Okaloosa Economic Development Council. As President of the Okaloosa EDC, Dr. Richburg got tired of seeing his community lose prospects to other communities that had more and better cultural amenities. What the community needed was a venue for providing activities and events in the fine and performing arts.

Never one to shy away from a challenge, Dr. Richburg decided that the community needed a fine and performing arts center that would compare favorably with the finest in the country. But there was a problem. The most conservative estimates at the time put the cost of such a facility at $20 million. Undaunted, Dr. Richburg had conceptual drawings developed and began selling his idea for a regional fine and performing arts center to decision makers locally and in the state capital.

There were a multitude of obstacles, roadblocks, and detours, but Dr. Richburg persevered and eventually was able to generate the support needed to secure the funding required to build a fine and performing arts complex that is widely acknowledged to be a showcase facility. As a result, a community that once lost prospects because it lacked cultural amenities now uses the symphony, Broadway plays, world-class art exhibits, the ballet, student performances, and other fine and performing arts activities as attractions when recruiting businesses from big city markets. This salutary change happened because a college president saw a civic problem and applied the principles of entrepreneurship to solve it.

Banker and Civic Entrepreneur

Jan Morgan is a banker who, while serving on the board of her community's local EDO, realized how difficult it was for new small businesses to secure start-up financing. Being an innovative civic entrepreneur, Morgan convinced the EDO's board to form a finance committee and agreed to chair it. Under Morgan's leadership, the Finance Committee developed a guide for small businesses entitled *How to Find Start-Up Funding in Johnson County.*

The committee also convinced local banks to develop a common loan application for small businesses so that entrepreneurs could complete one application and submit it to several banks simultaneously. Convincing her colleagues and competitors in banking that a common loan application made good business sense was difficult, but Jan Morgan is a true civic entrepreneur. It took her more than a year, but with perseverance and good natured stubbornness, Morgan eventually prevailed over all of the obstacles and got the job done.

Local Elected Official is a Civic Entrepreneur

Helen Peck is a county commissioner who risked her political future to help develop a badly needed industrial park in her community. Peck serves a community that has a high percentage of retired people who want things to stay just as they are. To them, economic development is a threat to why they retired in this particular community. The attitude of these retired citizens can be summarized as follows: "We are here—close the gate. No more growth." This attitude makes it difficult for the local EDO to create jobs for younger people in the community; a fact that becomes more of an issue everyday as the best and brightest must leave the community to find meaningful employment.

It took a referendum and a contested election to do it, but Peck finally convinced the voters in her community that an industrial park would be an asset. Peck's election opponent made the industrial park a high-profile campaign issue and attempted to rally the retired population in opposition to it. With the help of a coalition of business leaders and young people, Peck was able to convince the electorate of the need for an industrial park. She won both the election and the referendum.

Because of Helen Peck's civic entrepreneurship, there is now a thriving industrial park in the community that has attracted clean, high-tech firms which provide well-paying jobs for local residents. These jobs have, in turn, contributed so much to the local tax base that public services for all citizens—including the retired residents who opposed the industrial park—have improved noticeably.

Manufacturing Executive is a Civic Entrepreneur

Jason Lee is a manufacturing executive who saw a problem, decided to solve it, and in the process became a civic entrepreneur. While serving on the board of his local EDO, Lee became concerned about the financial problems faced by some of the community's smaller manufacturers.

These problems, in turn, led to retention and expansion problems. The community was losing too many of its small manufacturers to bankruptcy or relocation and those that were able to survive were unable to expand when opportunities presented themselves. Lee knew that many small firms experience financial difficulties simply because they are small. Because of their size, they are never able to achieve the economies of scale that are so helpful in boosting the bottom line for larger enterprises.

Lee had three reasons for wanting to help solve the retention and expansion problems associated with small manufacturers. First, Lee's company depended on some of these smaller firms to serve as subcontractors on its larger contracts. Second, Lee knew the CEOs of all of the smaller manufacturing firms and considered them not just colleagues, but friends. Finally, Lee knew the negative impact the loss of manufacturing jobs was having on the community.

To help solve the problem, Lee decided that the EDO needed to form a "collaborative manufacturing network." This network would enhance the EDO's efforts to retain and expand existing industry. The idea was to bring local manufacturers together in cooperative ventures that would help them achieve economy of scale and pursue contracts bigger than any of them could take on individually. His idea was to have smaller companies conduct joint marketing campaigns, offer joint training opportunities for employees, and form "teaming" partnerships for pursuing larger contracts. He also envisioned members of the network subcontracting work to other members instead of sending it to other companies outside of the community which was the normal practice.

It took more than three years to work through all of the obstacles, but the manufacturing network that Jason Lee envisioned is now an integral component of his local EDO's existing industry program. The most difficult obstacle faced by Lee and his fellow board members was resistance from the local manufacturing firms themselves; the very ones he was trying to help. When Lee first approached the manufacturing CEOs in his community with the idea of establishing a manufacturing network that would collaborate for the good of all, he ran head first into a brick wall of resistance.

The CEOs tended to view each other as competitors and thought the proposed network would just give their competitors some type of advantage. Breaking down the walls that separated the small manufacturers in the community required persuasion and perseverance. Lee had to show the CEOs that competition and cooperation did not have to be mutually exclusive concepts. They could compete when that approach was appropriate and collaborate when that approach was best. Using this logic, Lee was eventually able to gain the cooperation and support of the CEOs. Thanks to the civic entrepreneurship of one determined manufacturing executive, the network was established and all of its members have benefited from it.

These examples of civic entrepreneurship are just a few that demonstrate the contributions volunteer board members can make in the economic development of their communities. Community leaders and local elected officials who serve on the boards of local EDOs are the catalysts for and facilitators of economic development at the local level. They are civic entrepreneurs.

VISION AND THE CIVIC ENTREPRENEUR

Civic entrepreneurs look at their communities and see them not as they are but as they can be. Like all entrepreneurs, they focus on the possible and, by doing so, see opportunities where others see only problems. This salutary characteristic is known as "vision." Visionary people are creative thinkers and innovative problem solvers. To the civic entrepreneur with vision, obstacles that would frighten others away are simply hills to be climbed, potholes to be filled, and rivers to be crossed.

Consider this example of a civic entrepreneur with vision. Jack Jefferson was a banker and chairman of the board of his local EDO when disaster struck. In less than five years, the community's entire manufacturing base—which consisted solely of textile firms—closed down and moved off shore. Local leaders were frantic. Unemployment skyrocketed, lifelong residents moved away to find jobs in other towns, and the local tax base went into freefall.

At an emergency meeting of the local EDO's board, the mayor said, "Somebody better do something quick or this community is going to be a ghost town." While others wrung their hands and saw only the problems, Jack Jefferson saw opportunity. He led the EDO's board in a brainstorming session that focused on answering the following question: "Why would a company want to locate in our community?"

As board members stated their opinions, Jefferson wrote them on a flip chart. After more than an hour of brainstorming, the board had identified a number of positive attributes of their town:

- Good schools
- Slower pace of life
- Low crime rate
- Pleasant climate
- Within in an easy drive of a major city with a regional airport, university, and community college
- Plenty of land available for developing
- Easy access to an interstate highway

Jefferson took the pages from his flip chart to a graphic artist and had an attractive color brochure designed. He made the brochure the centerpiece of a marketing campaign to recruit new businesses to the community and to fill the buildings vacated by their former textiles tenants. He then contacted an executive in the home office of his bank and explained the challenge the community faced. What grew out of this discussion was an innovative marketing plan to attract firms currently operating in congested urban areas with high crime rates, high labor costs, unpleasant weather, and poor quality schools.

It took several years for the marketing plan to bear fruit—economic development can be a slow-moving enterprise—but once the first company relocated to the town, others followed. The community's once vacant buildings are now fully occupied. The town's tax base has been restored, and homes that were boarded up and vacant now house families again. A desperate situation was turned around because one civic entrepreneur had the vision to see beyond the problems of today to the possibilities of tomorrow.

LEADERSHIP AND THE CIVIC ENTREPRENEUR

There are as many different definitions of leadership as there are fields of endeavor calling for good leadership. Leadership has been defined from the perspectives of business, sports, the military, religion, and other fields. Although the various definitions share a set of common elements, they also have distinguishing features relating to the specific field in question. Such is the case for the following definition of leadership:

> *Leadership, as it relates to civic entrepreneurship, is the ability to persuade others to put aside personal agendas and make a full commitment to pursuing goals that are in the best interests of the overall community.*

In any community, there will be those who support economic development and those who don't. There will be those who favor a certain type of development, but oppose others types. There will be those who will support selected economic development projects as long as they are not in their neighborhood. Most people operate on the basis of self-interest and few things will reveal those interests faster or more clearly than economic development.

Civic entrepreneurs exercise leadership when they are able to bring people with differing interests and conflicting agendas together and persuade them to work cooperatively for the greater good of the overall community. As chairman of the board for his local EDO, Tom Mathews saw a need to expand the organization's funding base. Financial constraints were holding the EDO back from undertaking important projects that would benefit the community. Historically, the EDO had operated solely on the support of private funds raised by charging membership dues. Mathews knew that in order to expand the EDO's budget sufficiently to make it a real player, he would have to secure public funding. But there was a problem. Two members of the local county commission—the body that would provide public funding—were adamantly opposed to using tax dollars to support economic development. They viewed this practice as "corporate welfare."

Mathews decided to meet with the two commissioners and try to show them that public funding of economic development, if handled properly, is an investment not a handout. They agreed to meet with him, but after more than an hour of fruitless debate, Mathews saw that he needed a different approach. Out of desperation and on the spur of the moment, Mathews said, "Our EDO will contract with the County to increase the local tax base." He went on to explain that at least ten percent of the financial benefit induced by economic development returns to the county in the form of taxes. When he told the reluctant commissioners that just $500,000 of induced economic activity in a given year would return approximately $50,000 to the county in taxes, the wall of resistance he had been knocking his head against began to crumble.

After a little more discussion, the reluctant commissioners became believers. Once the details had been negotiated, a contract was drawn up and the EDO received its first public funds. Mathews is no longer chairman of the board, but he certainly made his mark while serving in that office. Thanks to his leadership, the EDO is now a public-private partnership that maintains a 50-50 ratio between public and private funding. Its budget and the corresponding number of projects that can be undertaken have both doubled. The contract to expand the community's tax base has been a win-win undertaking for the EDO and the county.

CIVIC ENTREPRENEURSHIP AND ECONOMIC DEVELOPMENT

The volunteers who serve in leadership positions in local EDOs are civic entrepreneurs. Their role in economic development involves establishing a vision for the community, bringing together the groups and individuals whose participation and cooperation are necessary in order to achieve the vision, and undertaking economic development projects aimed at fulfilling the vision. Their role also involves persuading all stakeholders to cooperate for the greater good of the overall community, setting the strategic direction for the local EDO, and ensuring that sufficient funding is available to support economic development. To do these things, civic entrepreneurs have to exhibit all of the characteristics of a business entrepreneur: vision, self-motivation, positive attitude, unconventional thinking, persuasiveness, leadership, perseverance, and consensus building.

Chapter One

███
███

OVERVIEW OF ECONOMIC DEVELOPMENT

CHAPTER OUTLINE

- Economic development defined
- Purpose of economic development
- Sustainable economic development
- Capacity building in economic development
- Effect of economic development on a community
- Critical factors and their effect on economic development

As a volunteer LEADER for a local economic development organization (EDO), you do not have to be an economic development professional. However, the more you understand about economic development, the more effective you will be in fulfilling your responsibilities as a board member for your local EDO. This chapter provides the foundation upon which you can build an understanding of the basics of economic development. Community leaders who understand the material presented in this chapter as well as the rest of the book will be better prepared to participate intelligently and effectively in the on-going economic development of their communities.

ECONOMIC DEVELOPMENT DEFINED

Whenever the topic of conversation is economic development, you are likely to hear a variety of terms. It has been my experience that community leaders are often confused by the various terms people use to describe the concept of economic development. Some of the more commonly used of these terms are *community development, industrial development,* and *business development.* These terms all represent concepts that are subsets of the broader concept of economic development. To prevent confusion relating to terminology, I will begin with some definitions.

Economic development is the process whereby communities mobilize their human, financial, physical, and natural resources in order to: 1) create and retain jobs, 2) improve their economy, and 3) enhance their quality of life. As part of its overall economic development program, a local EDO might engage in community, industrial, and/or business development.

Community development is the process local EDO's undertake to improve the quality of life in a given locality. This is why community development is sometimes referred to as "locality development." For example, downtown redevelopment programs fall into this subset of economic development. Typical goals of community development programs are a more attractive appearance, enhanced safety, more and better cultural and recreational opportunities, and more conducive gathering places.

Industrial development is the process local EDO's undertake to attract, expand, and/or home-grow industrial businesses such as manufacturing and processing. Because industrial businesses tend to provide higher paying jobs and bring money into the community from the outside by exporting their products, industrial development is often a major focus of local EDOs; especially that aimed at building a base of high-tech firms.

Business development is the process local EDOs undertake to bring more businesses to their community or to home-grow them. It is similar to industrial development except that it focuses on non-industrial businesses. The goal of business development is to continually improve the economy of a community through improved profitability and competitiveness for existing businesses and the job creation associated with new and expanding businesses.

A local EDO, depending on its size and composition, might be simultaneously engaged in community, industrial, and business development; all under the broad umbrella of economic development. However, of these three types of economic development programs, local EDOs are more likely to be engaged in business and industrial development than in community development. Because community development programs typically focus on such things as community pride, establishing a unique community identity, beautification projects, festivals, and culture/leisure related activities, they often become the responsibility of chambers of commerce or stand-alone, single-focus organizations.

PURPOSES OF ECONOMIC DEVELOPMENT

Why do communities form EDOs in the first place? What are they trying to accomplish? The answers to these questions can be found in the purposes economic development can serve for a community. Prominent among these purposes are: 1) enhancing the quality of life, 2) improving the economy, 3) stabilizing economic ups and downs, 4) diversifying the types of jobs available as well as the overall economy, 5) increasing the overall per capita income level, 6) creating more and better jobs, and 7) managing the rate and type of growth.

All of these purposes are positive and desirable. After all, what community would not want a better quality of life; stable, growing, diversified economy; and more and high-paying jobs? The good news is that if undertaken effectively, economic development can achieve any or all of these purposes. However, local economic development has an Achilles heel: the tendency of people to always want more and want it right now.

This tendency can cause the leaders of local EDOs to make short-sighted decisions that lead to long-term problems; something that you as a volunteer leader must guard against. One of your most important responsibilities as a volunteer leader is to insulate your EDO's economic development professionals from the predictable pressures to pursue short-sighted development projects. Examples of local EDOs making decisions that pay off in the short-term but cause problems later abound in economic development. Just a few examples will illustrate this unfortunate but common phenomenon:

- Under pressure from several county commissioners who are up for reelection and anxious to show results, a local EDO bends its rules and allows a minimum-wage paying company to locate in its industrial park. The decision will show an immediate gain of more than 200 jobs, but they are not the type or quality of jobs the community needs. To make matters worse, the EDO has now squandered a valuable piece of property that will not be put to its highest and best use; a tract of land that could have housed a high-wage business if the EDO had just waited.

- A community with a tourism-based economy—the central asset of which is a beautiful lake surrounded by a quiet, tranquil forest spotted with cabins and campsites—over-develops and, in the process, transforms the lake into an urban center of condominiums, over-crowded shops, and grid-locked traffic. This community is like the farmer who, because his appetite cannot be satisfied, eventually eats his seed corn.

- One member of a local EDO's board pressures his colleagues to pursue an economic development project that will be good for his company, but bad for the community. Worn down by his strong-arm tactics and persistent lobbying, the board agrees to pursue his project; a fact the EDO and community will come to regret.

These are just three examples of many that could be cited to illustrate how human nature can intervene to the detriment of responsible economic development. In every case, the volunteer leaders of the local EDO could have stood firm against what they knew were bad decisions, but chose not to. The broad goal of any EDO should be sustainable economic development, and it is the responsibility of volunteers to ensure that this goal is not undermined by human nature.

SUSTAINABLE ECONOMIC DEVELOPMENT

As was illustrated in the previous section, short-term thinking leads to short-term results; results that are likely to be overshadowed by the problems they cause in the long run. This is why it is important for community leaders who serve as volunteer leaders in local EDOs to stay focused themselves and, in turn, keep the EDO focused on sustainable economic development.

Sustainable economic development is development that meets the needs of the community in the present without compromising the future. Examples of economic development that could not be sustained abound in regions where the economy was once based solely on non-renewable resources such as coal, copper, gold, or diamond mining. There are many examples in which over-mining combined with a failure to diversify turned once thriving boom towns into ghost towns. Similar examples may be found in regions with timber, oil, and tourism-based economies.

Sustainable economic development occurs when community leaders establish a long-term vision, when they focus not just on the community's non-renewable resources but also on its renewable resources, and when they consider both the short and long-term consequences of their decisions. This is easy to say, but hard to do as you will surely learn before you have served for very long on a local EDO's board. However, even though focusing on sustainable economic development can be a challenge, it is a challenge that must be met if your community is going to prosper in the long run.

CAPACITY BUILDING IN ECONOMIC DEVELOPMENT

Another critical responsibility of community leaders who serve as volunteer leaders for local EDOs is to keep the organization from putting the cart before the horse. This happens when boards allow themselves to be pressured into trying to produce immediate results; an ever-present threat to most boards. Putting the cart before the horse in the current context means pursuing economic development projects the community is not yet capable of handling. For example, rural communities that form an EDO one day and then try to hit a home run the next by attracting a major manufacturing plant are putting the cart before the horse.

Major manufacturing plants have enormous needs for water, electricity, gas, skilled labor, and other necessities. If the community does not yet have the capacity to provide for these needs, it is putting the cart before the horse when it tries to recruit a major manufacturing plant. Communities prepare themselves to be successful in economic development through capacity building.

Capacity, in the context of economic development, means the ability of a community to provide for the needs of the businesses it recruits, expands, or home-grows. Economic development capacity consists of three basic elements: 1) Commitment on the part of the community, those who fund economic development, and those who lead local EDOs; 2) Sufficient assets, resources, and support services in place to accommodate the businesses recruited, expanded, or home grown; and 3) A well-run local EDO to lead, coordinate, and facilitate the community's economic development efforts.

To illustrate how even well-intended communities can get ahead of themselves with regard to capacity, consider this example from my past. I once worked as a consultant for a rural community that attempted to recruit a major manufacturing firm within just weeks of establishing its EDO. When my attempts to encourage capacity building fell on deaf ears, I decided to step out of the way and let the community's EDO learn the hard way; which it did in short order. The company in question was looking for a location that could provide a "turnkey site;" one that already had all utilities available at the street and all other needs in place and ready to go. All my client community could offer was virgin acreage that had not even been cleared. As soon as the company learned of this situation, the community was quickly scratched from its list of potential sites.

A good rule of thumb to remember as a board member for a local EDO is this: *capacity building first—economic development second.* To pursue economic development projects before the community has the capacity to support them is like building a house without first laying a foundation. This does not necessarily mean that everything needs to be in place before beginning to recruit businesses. Often, some of the tasks that must be completed for capacity-building and recruiting can be undertaken in parallel. But timing is critical. A company that wants to be operational in six months is not going to wait while a community rushes to build an industrial park that will require at least two years to complete. Consequently, as a board member for a local EDO, you will want to ensure that sufficient progress is made on capacity building before initiating major development efforts.

EFFECT OF ECONOMIC DEVELOPMENT ON A COMMUNITY

Justifying the cost of economic development is a never-ending challenge for community leaders who serve as volunteer leaders of local EDOs. Volunteers and practitioners are often asked to show in tangible terms how an investment in economic development will pay off. The problem is not that well-planned and effectively implemented economic development projects don't produce tangible results; they do.

Rather, it is that often the results of investments in economic development made today will not be seen until much later, and funding providers—being human—want to see an immediate return on their investment. Because you are likely to hear the question so often, it is important that you be able to articulate the effects of economic development on a community.

Effect of Economic Development on a Community

The most widely-used measures of economic development at the local level are jobs created, earnings, output (sales), and tax revenue. Consider what happens in a community when a new business locates there or an existing business expands its operations. In order to generate new or additional output, the business must hire employees and purchase materials. These employees earn income and spend it on living costs, recreation, leisure, education, and other expenses.

The business spends some of its corporate earnings on the resources needed to generate additional output. These two phenomena—personal and corporate spending—increase sales, employment, and earnings in other sectors of the community's economy. In addition, the business and its employees pay sales, ad valorem, corporate, and other taxes, as appropriate, that support local government services.

The most obvious effects of economic development on a community are, of course, economic. However, economic development can also have a positive effect on the social and political structure of a community. Communities benefit economically from the new jobs, increased sales, enhanced earning and—in turn—spending, and a broader/deeper tax base. They also benefit from the increased productivity of land and buildings that occurs when previously unused sites are leased or purchased by a business.

The social benefits of economic development to a community include fewer citizens on public assistance and a decrease in such problems as unemployment, crime, and poverty, as well as the spin-off problems associated with them. More people working in a community and at better jobs also leads to more political stability. The sense of purpose, pride, identity, and self-sufficiency people can gain from working in well-paying jobs tend to stabilize the political environment of the community.

On the other hand, all is not necessarily gain in economic development, and you need to understand the potential down side of the concept well enough to help avoid it. Just as you would with any potential contract in your business, you—as a board member of your local EDO—should look carefully at the cost/benefit ratio of any potential economic development project before encouraging the organization to pursue it. The potential costs of economic development projects can extend well beyond the more obvious direct costs.

New businesses will make new demands on the community's infrastructure. Roads can become over-crowded, the water supply can be over-taxed, and the solid waste/sewer infrastructure can be over-subscribed. The environment can suffer. Quiet, rural settings can be transformed into crowded residential neighborhoods. Recreational facilities can be over-used and educational systems enrolled beyond their limits.

Not all members of a community will support economic development. This is why it is so important that you be able to articulate the positive effects of economic development on a community and lead your local EDO in such a way that the community gains the good while minimizing the bad. In the long run, if the citizens of a community do not support economic development, the EDO and all of its efforts will ultimately fail.

CRITICAL FACTORS AND THEIR EFFECT ON ECONOMIC DEVELOPMENT

There are many reasons why businesses considering a relocation or expansion choose a given community, and it is important for you to understand these reasons; but first, some terminology. When a business is considering a relocation or expansion, but has no particular community in mind, it is known in economic development circles as a "suspect." If this same business decides to consider your community as a potential location, it becomes a "prospect."

The most common reasons businesses select a given community fall into one or more of the following categories: raw materials, transportation, market proximity, workforce/brainpower, capital, energy, water, climate, environment, community factors, land, and education. The availability of relocation incentives is also an important factor, but one that typically comes into play only after the more fundamental factors in the categories just listed have been satisfied.

Raw Materials

Sometimes the availability of raw materials will enhance a community's economic development potential. Businesses that depend on certain raw materials always face the dilemma of whether to locate near the raw materials or near the market for their products. In solving this dilemma, businesses are often guided by the answers to two questions: 1) Does the raw material lose or gain weight during processing? and 2) Is the raw material perishable?

Generally speaking, a community's raw materials are more of an attraction if they lose a substantial amount of weight during processing. This rule of thumb can be attributed to the cost of shipping. When raw materials lose a substantial amount of weight during processing, it is less expensive to transport the finished product to market than to transport the heavier raw materials to processing plants. When a business transports raw materials that lose a substantial amount of weight during processing, they are paying to ship waste material.

Consequently, in such cases the business is more likely to locate near the heavy raw materials and ship the lighter finished products to the market. An example of this situation would be a lumber company that locates a saw mill near the source of the trees and ships the finished lumber to its various markets, thereby saving on transportation costs.

A community can expect its raw materials to have a strong attraction if they perish rapidly or do not travel well. Because of advances in refrigeration and shipping technology, perishability is less of a factor that it once was. However, there still times when it comes into play. For example, although refrigerated air transportation makes it possible to ship seafood and milk anywhere in the world overnight, seafood processing plants and dairies are still typically located close to the source of the raw materials.

Transportation

Transportation can be an important factor when a business makes a location decision. The transportation system—be it road, rail, air, or sea—is what ties a business to its suppliers and customers. Businesses that depend on a certain mode of transportation in order to receive materials from suppliers and deliver products to their markets must locate in areas that have access to that mode of transportation.

Jackson County, Florida is an instructive example of how important access to transportation can be as an economic development asset. Jackson County offers access to an east-west Interstate highway, a major north-south roadway, a railhead near the Interstate highway, and direct access to an airport and seaport. Access to these various forms of transportation has allowed the Jackson County Development Council to transform this sparsely populated, rural county in northwest Florida into an economic development success story by attracting transportation-intensive businesses and locating them in thematic industrial and business parks.

Market Proximity

Advances in transportation technology and systems have decreased the importance of market proximity as an economic development asset. However, for certain types of businesses, it is still an important factor. Businesses that distribute high-volume, high-weight, high-value products—products that are expensive and often hazardous to transport—tend to locate in close proximity to their market. For example, businesses that manufacture yachts tend to locate near their market or at least near the water because of the high cost and hazards associated with shipping yachts.

Workforce and Brainpower

Workforce is always an important economic development asset. Communities that have a well-trained workforce readily available in sufficient numbers and at competitive wages will always make the short list when businesses are making location decisions. This is especially the case if the workforce is non-unionized and has a positive work ethic. For example, many of the businesses that have located in Okaloosa County, Florida did so at least partially because of the availability of young retired military personnel from the County's three Air Force Bases: Eglin, Hurlburt, and Duke. Retired Air Force personnel are known to be well-trained, mature, self-motivated, and possessed of a positive work ethic and non-union perspective; attractive attributes for businesses making location decisions.

Brainpower is also an economic development asset. Certain types of businesses such as high technology, research, and engineering firms need well educated, highly skilled personnel. Consequently, communities that are known to have outstanding school systems, community colleges, colleges, and/or universities that graduate well-prepared students are typically inviting locations for firms that are education intensive.

Capital

The ability to provide financial assistance locally is an important economic development asset for communities. The availability and cost of capital will both be important factors to businesses making location decisions. The availability of local venture capital or the ability to connect businesses with venture capitalists can also be important. Local communities should be prepared to discuss the following types of financial assistance with businesses that are making location decisions: 1) direct loans from local business development corporations, banks, and private investors; 2) state loans and loan guarantee programs; 3) federal loans and loan guarantees; 4) municipal and/or industrial bond financing programs; and 5) local and state financial incentive programs including tax breaks and deferred payment plans.

Energy

Access to dependable, competitively priced energy is an economic development asset for communities. This is especially the case when dealing with energy-intensive prospects such as manufacturing and processing firms. Even businesses that are less energy-intensive will want to know what types of energy are available and at what rates. Energy-intensive businesses will also be interested in the stability of energy rates in the community. An erratic graph of unpredictable ups and downs in energy rates is the worst-case scenario from the prospect's point of view; worse even than high rates. In fact, high rates that are stable and predictable are actually better than unpredictable rates—not good, but better. This is because in order for a company to develop a realistic business plan containing accurate projections, energy rates must be predictable over time.

Water

Although water is an important resource for any business, it is often taken for granted. However, for certain types of businesses, water is so essential that an insufficient supply of it can be a deal killer. For example, certain types of companies such as microchip manufacturres use so much water that they must be shown that it will be dependably available in the required amounts. Important factors that are considered by water-intensive businesses are: current water supply, projected supplies, commercial/industrial rates, peak-use periods, low-demand periods, and quality/contamination data.

Climate

Climate can be an economic development asset or liability for a community. Of course, a community cannot choose its climate, but it can take advantage what it has or work to mitigate the negative aspects of what it doesn't. The impact of climate on tourism and agriculture is obvious. Either a community has the right climate for these business sectors or it doesn't. However, the impact of climate on other sectors such as manufacturing and services may not be so obvious. In these sectors the impact is indirect.

Perhaps the most important impact of the climate is on productivity; a factor that is affected by the average number of work days per year. For example, a company in Albany, New York might see its productivity numbers suffer because of the absenteeism, tardiness, and down days associated with snow storms. This same company located in a region with a milder climate might experience less absenteeism/tardiness and no down days. Heating, cooling, and insurance costs must also be considered by businesses locating in regions with extreme climates.

For example, businesses that locate in Florida benefit from the fact that in most years employees are able to get to work 365 days a year. On the other hand, hurricanes can quickly and unpredictably change this desirable situation while at the same time driving up insurance costs. This is why it is important to know the benefits and liabilities of your region's climate and how these factors will be perceived by different types of businesses.

Environment

For the most part, federal and state regulations have leveled the economic development playing field between communities when it comes to environmental considerations. This is because the cost of complying with environmental regulations will be approximately the same from community to community except in those cases in which local communities have passed statutes that are stricter than state and federal guidelines.

Environmental regulations can be an economic development asset or liability depending on the type of business in question. Businesses that produce toxic waste or potentially harmful products will avoid communities that emphasize the environment as an economic development asset. In fact, the trend is for this type of company to locate off shore as a way to avoid strict environmental regulation. On the other hand, there are businesses that will view an environmental emphasis as an asset when making location decisions. The key is for your EDO to focus on attracting the types of businesses that are suited to your community's environmental philosophy.

Community Factors

Community considerations can be important when businesses are making location decisions. This is why community development can be so important to business development. In fact, it is not uncommon for community factors to tip the balance in a community's favor against it when negotiating with prospects. Community factors include a variety of amenities that may or may not directly affect a prospect such as cultural activities, attitudes of community leaders, quality of the education system, available services, recreational activities, incentive programs, and community appearance.

Cultural, recreational, and educational considerations are often important to prospects because they can make it easier or more difficult to recruit and retain a high-value workforce. Community appearance can be important for the same reasons. A well-maintained, attractive community can be helpful to company officials who must uproot their families and key personnel in order to relocate their business. If a community makes a good visual impression, company officials will have less difficulty convincing their families and those of key personnel to make the move.

A critical community factor is attitude. Prospects must feel welcome and wanted by local elected officials, business leaders, and the community at large. Prospects will sense the community's attitude and make note of it. Are community leaders open, warm, and welcoming or guarded and cold? Do community leaders go out of their way to help or just respond minimally as necessary? The best asset a community can have when all other factors are equal is a positive, welcoming attitude that says: "We are glad you have come and hope you will stay."

Land

Available and inexpensive land is typically an economic development asset for communities. In fact, the cost of land is often given more consideration by prospects than it should be considering that it is a one-time purchase and can be amortized over a number of years. Typically, prospects will want land that is level, available in large enough tracts to accommodate future expansion, and inexpensive. Prospects typically want to know the cost per unit of land, location, availability of utilities, state of development, and how much room exists for future expansion.

Of these various concerns, the state of development is almost always high on a prospect's list. A fully developed industrial, commerce, or technology park with available land at reasonable prices is one of the best economic development assets a community can have. Showing prospects undeveloped land is not usually nearly as effective a strategy as showing them a fully-developed, turnkey site. If the site comes with a suitable facility, it is an even better asset. This is why some EDOs go to the expense of building a "spec" building (a building that is built based on the speculation that if we build it they will come).

Education

Education is almost always an important factor in location decisions. Prospects will be interested in education from several different perspectives. Prospects typically ask the following or similar questions about education: Can the education system prepare the workforce we need? Can the education system provide on-going training for our employees? Can the education system provide customized in-house training? Is quality education available for the children of our personnel? Is there a community college or university nearby? What types of programs are available in these institutions? Do these institutions have an established record of working well with local businesses?

It is important for the board members of local EDOs to understand that prospects will view education from both a personal and professional point of view. They will want to know that education and training are available for their personnel, but they will also want to know that quality education is available for their children and those of their personnel.

Relocation Incentives

Relocation incentives, when used as an economic development tool, are often misunderstood and almost always controversial. Do they represent what must be done in order to play in today's competitive arena, or are they just a form of corporate welfare? Ironically, the answer to both parts of this question can be "yes." The same incentive package can be a deciding factor in one situation and a waste of money in another. In some cases, relocation incentives will be critical in a prospect's final relocation decision. In other cases, they are little more than money given away unnecessarily. The key to ensuring the former and avoiding the latter is to have a formal plan for determining when to offer relocation incentives and what requirements come with the incentives.

A community's relocation incentives plan should have two components. The first should contain specific criteria a business must meet in order to qualify for incentives. The second should contain performance requirements a business will have to meet over time in order to actually receive the incentives it qualifies for. In developing such a plan, it is important for the EDO to bring all stakeholders to the table. This means conducting focus groups that include the EDO's board, local government officials, education officials, and community leaders from all applicable sectors.

Criteria for Qualifying Businesses to Receive Relocation Incentives

The criteria adopted for qualifying businesses to receive relocation criteria will vary from community to community depending on circumstances and priorities. In fact, they can vary from year to year within the same community. The following questions will help you and your colleagues on the local EDO's board develop criteria that fit your community's specific circumstances and priorities:

- Will the number of jobs created by the business justify the incentives?
- Will the wages paid by the business justify the incentives?
- Will the business produce high-value products or provide high-value services?
- Will the businesses presence tend to improve the quality of life in the community in the long run?

- Will the business create jobs for low-income/high-unemployment groups in the community?

- Is the business committed to the community for the long run?

- Will the business create new increase sales for other local businesses?

- Does the business have a record of being a good corporate neighbor?

These types of questions will help a community decide whether or not a given business is a worthy candidate for relocation incentives. Of course, the more questions such as these that receive an affirmative response, the better. Whether or not all such questions must be answered "yes" depends on the community's circumstances, priorities, and preferences. This is a local decision that you, as an EDO volunteer, might have to help make.

Performance Criteria for Receiving Incentives

It is one thing for a business to qualify for relocation incentives, but quite another for it to follow through and comply with all applicable criteria. To ensure that results match promises when awarding relocation incentives, local EDOs should develop performance criteria and pay incentives based on actual performance in much the same way that a bank pays its "draws" to a building contractor.

The recommended approach is a written contract in which relocation incentives are tied to specific performance criteria. For example, if a company agrees that it will hire 100 local people at a specified average wage, the portion of the relocation incentives tied to this criterion would be paid only when the company made good on its promise. This means that contracts for relocation incentives should contain a cancellation clause that allows the EDO to cancel certain incentives or even all incentives for failure to perform.

The contract should also contain a recovery clause that allows the EDO to recover incentives or portions of incentives if the business fails to comply for the specified period of time or to the specified level. The contract should contain a penalty clause which the EDO may invoke should the business relocate before a specified period of time has elapsed. Finally, the contract should contain an adjustment clause that allows the EDO to make adjustments to accommodate changing circumstances or unexpected conditions.

Local EDOs that approach the concept of relocation incentives objectively, apply well-conceived qualifying and performance criteria systematically, and award their incentives wisely can turn them into good investments that will pay dividends in the long run. However, communities that get caught up in the "we-have-to-offer-incentives-because-everyone-else-does" mentality and award them unwisely may eventually lose more than they gain.

I saw first hand what can happen when a local EDO awards relocation incentives without first developing well-thought-out qualifying and performance incentives. I was hired as a consultant to help a community that was working to recruit a textile manufacturing firm to replace one the community had lost. Against my advice, the local EDO arranged to provide a building at no cost for one year, give the company in question a five-year tax break, and award several other relocation incentives.

The company relocated to the community in question, set up operations, collected its incentives, and ten months later relocated to another community that was also naïve enough to award incentives with no strings attached. After doing a little research for my EDO client, I discovered that this company had a long record of moving from town to town as a way to avoid the normal cost of doing business. In fact, the company had the pack-up-and-move routine down to a science. In one night—it usually left at night—the company could pack all of its equipment onto a truck and be gone before morning. Then it could be operational within 24 hours of arriving at its new destination.

With the foundation provided in this chapter, you are now prepared to learn the more specific information presented in the remaining chapters. Each chapter in the remainder of this book explains what you need to know about a specific aspect of economic development in order to be an effective volunteer leader in a local EDO.

Chapter Two

███
███

THE VOLUNTEER BOARD MEMBER: ROLES AND RESPONSIBILITIES

CHAPTER OUTLINE

- Governance in local EDOs
- Characteristics of effective board members
- Responsibilities of EDO boards
- Legal obligations of EDO boards
- Operating documents of EDO boards
- Liability and EDO boards
- Ground rules for board members
- Potential legal issues for EDO boards
- Strategic direction and the EDO board
- Leadership and the EDO board

The majority of local EDOs are public-private partnerships legally structured as not-for-profit corporations. The actual legal structure of the EDO might be a 501(c) (3), 501 (c) (6), or exempt organization as defined by the Internal Revenue Service. Regardless of the actual legal structure adopted, not-for-profit organizations are governed by a board of directors. Serving on the board is one of the most important functions a volunteer leader can perform in a local EDO. In the case of local EDOs, the board of directors is typically comprised of volunteer community leaders drawn from the organization's membership and local elected officials.

GOVERNANCE IN ECONOMIC DEVELOPMENT

Local EDOs typically operate on the corporate model. This means that governance is provided by the organization's board of directors while management is provided by an economic development professional and his or her staff. The CEO typically has the title "President and CEO," but some EDOs still use the not-for-profit model in which the CEO has the title "executive Director." It is important that, as a board member for your local EDO, you understand the distinction between governance and management. This is often an area of contention in EDOs because board members are typically managers in their own businesses and professions.

As managers, they tend to view the world from a management perspective. Consequently, when serving as a board member responsible for governance rather than management, some civic entrepreneurs cannot resist the temptation to push the economic development professionals aside and try to manage the organization themselves. This is a mistake. What follows are some shorthand statements that are widely used to describe the distinction between governance and management:

- The board makes policy (governance)—the staff implements it (management).
- The board governs—the staff manages.
- The board is strategic—the staff is operational.

In the more effective EDOs, the board and staff work together in a mutually-supportive partnership in which each partner understands and accepts its assigned role. Board members avoid the temptation to micromanage the staff, and staff members avoid the temptation to dictate policy to the board.

CHARACTERISTICS OF EFFECTIVE BOARD MEMBERS

The quality of a local EDO's board, more than any other factor, will determine the effectiveness of the organization. Even the most dedicated staff led by the most talented economic development professional can take the local EDO no farther than the vision of its board. With very few exceptions, effective EDOs have effective boards. Consequently, volunteers who serve on the boards of local EDOs need to understand what makes a board effective.

As a volunteer board member and economic development consultant, I have worked with numerous local EDOs and their boards. Regardless of the size of the board and regardless of the demographics of the community, the boards that are the most effective share a number of common characteristics. Effective boards are:

- Partnership-oriented
- Visionary
- Independent-minded, critical thinkers
- Transparent
- Good stewards of local resources
- Value-oriented

Partnership-Oriented

Although the boards and staffs of local EDOs have different responsibilities—boards govern and staffs manage—boards are most effective when they work in a mutually-supportive way with the organization's chief executive. The relationship of an EDO board and its chief executive is symbiotic in that each party is dependent on the other and neither is able to fully carry out its duties in the absence of mutual cooperation.

Visionary

The most effective EDO boards are comprised of visionary members who look into the future and establish a strategic direction for the organization that is based on what is possible. In addition to establishing a vision that is part of a strategic plan (covered later), boards establish a comprehensive set of corporate values for the EDO. These corporate values are used as guiding principles—a framework within which the board and staff function as they work together to achieve the EDO's mission and fulfill its vision.

Independent-Minded Critical Thinkers

People who just go along to get along make ineffective board members for local EDOs. The best board members are those who can work in partnership with the staff and other board members without losing their intellectual independence. Independent-minded board members are critical thinkers who strain all input through a filter of common sense, experience, intuition, the EDO's corporate values, and what is best for the community. This characteristic is important because there will be people, organizations, and agencies in the community who will approach the EDO with proposals that serve their individual needs or agendas, but not those of the EDO or the overall community.

Transparent

Transparency means conducting the EDO's business in the sunshine so to speak. This characteristic is the opposite of making secret decisions in some smoked-filled rooms to which only a select few have access. Even those EDOs that receive no public funding should operate in the sunshine because stakeholders know what the EDO is doing as well as where, when, why, and how. Transparency promotes integrity and integrity builds trust.

This is important because an EDO's stakeholders must be able to trust its board members to conduct themselves according to the highest ethical standards and in ways that serve something bigger than self— namely the community. Another aspect of transparency is to remember that, as a board member, you should never surprise the EDO's stakeholders. Springing surprises on the community served by the EDO is a sure way to lose the support of stakeholders.

Stewardship

The best board members are good stewards of the resources entrusted to their care. These resources include all physical, financial, and human resources that are the responsibility of the EDO. Remember, these resources include all of those community resources that make it an attractive location in the first place. In practical terms, being a good steward translates into such specific actions as the following:

- Careful oversight of the EDO's budget
- Appropriate care and maintenance of the EDO's facilities
- Ensuring that the EDO is led and managed by a competent, dedicated economic development professional.
- Ensuring that economic development is managed in a way that protects and maintains what makes the community an attractive location.

Value Orientation

The best board members for local EDOs have a value orientation. This means that they approach their responsibilities in ways that ensure the EDO adds value to the community. In order to add value to the community, EDOs must understand what their stakeholders value; what they think is important. A retirement community that values a quiet, serene environment will not value economic development projects that create hustle and bustle, crowding, and noise. On the other hand, a community that values high-paying jobs for its younger residents will expect more from its EDO than just a few fast food restaurants and service businesses.

RESPONSIBILITIES OF EDO BOARD MEMBERS

Board members of local EDOs are responsible for setting the strategic direction for the organization and developing appropriate policies that support that direction. These broad responsibilities can be broken down more specifically as follows:

- Developing and adopting a comprehensive strategic plan for the organization that includes a vision, mission, corporate values, and broad strategic goals.

- Hiring a competent, dedicated economic development professional to lead and manage the day-to-day operations of the EDO as its CEO.

- Establishing specific performance goals for the CEO, monitoring performance regularly, and evaluating performance periodically.

- Ensuring that the EDO has sufficient resources to carry out its responsibilities (funding, facilities, technology, staff, volunteers, and community support).

- Providing good stewardship to ensure that the EDO's resources are used efficiently and effectively.

- Monitoring the EDO's recruiting, retention, and other development projects and programs to ensure their effectiveness.

- Promoting a positive image for the EDO in the community.

- Ensuring accountability—fiscal, legal, and ethical.

- Conducting self-evaluations of the board's effectiveness and take appropriate action to continually improve its effectiveness.

- Electing the EDO's officers (e.g. board chair, secretary, treasurer, etc.).

- Assisting the organization's CEO in maintaining positive relations with local elected officials, government agencies and their senior staff personnel, and other funding providers.

- Identifying, recruiting, and orienting new board members as appropriate.

The more effectively board members carry out these responsibilities, the more effective the EDO will be in carrying out its mission.

LEGAL OBLIGATIONS OF EDO BOARDS

Volunteers who serve on the boards of local EDOs assume certain legal obligations. The most important of these obligations are as follows:

- Duty of care
- Duty of loyalty
- Duty of obedience

Duty of Care

Should a legal challenge arise concerning actions or decisions of the local EDO's board, the first legal principle that will be applied by the court is the *duty of care*. This principle will be posed as a question. Did board members exercise reasonable care when making the decision or taking the action in question? What this principle really means in practical terms is that board members have a legal obligation to apply good judgement when acting on behalf of the EDO.

Duty of Loyalty

This principle is more commonly as the *conflict of interest* principle. Volunteer board members of local EDOs should avoid even the appearance of conflict of interest when making decisions on behalf of the organization. For example, assume that a banker is a board member of the local EDO. The issue before the board is selecting a bank to handle the EDO's accounts for the next five years. The banker who is a voting member of the board clearly has a conflict of interest.

To avoid the conflict, the banker should ask that the minutes of the board meeting show that he or she neither voted nor participated in the discussion leading to the vote on this issue. Another option would be for the banker to recommend that the EDO make its selection on the basis of a competitive bid. Even if this approach is taken, the banker would still want to recuse himself from all discussions and votes relating to the selection.

Duty of Obedience

This principle requires compliance on the part of board members with the EDO's by-laws, articles of incorporation, policies, and approved operational procedures. Compliance also applies more broadly applicable legal and ethical guidelines. It is important for board members to make a point of knowing the details of the EDO's by-laws, articles of incorporation, policies, and procedures. From a legal perspective, ignorance is not a viable defense.

OPERATING DOCUMENTS OF EDO BOARDS

A local EDO is like any other corporation in that it should have certain operating documents. At a minimum these documents should include the following:

1. Articles of incorporation (if the EDO is a not-for-profit corporation or an exempt organization of any kind as defined by the Internal Revenue System)
2. By-laws
3. Financial statement (produced on a monthly basis by the staff)
4. Minutes of all board meetings
5. Policy manual
6. Strategic plan that is reviewed annually and updated as necessary

Each of these documents is a tool that will help board members fulfill the legal obligations and board responsibilities explained earlier in this chapter.

LIABILITY AND EDO BOARDS

Volunteers should understand the ramifications of serving on the board of a local EDO. There are potential liabilities. Most state legislatures extend a certain level of immunity to volunteer board members of civic and charitable organizations, but the level can vary from state to state. Consequently, the best way volunteers can protect themselves from law suits relating to their service on an EDO board is to: 1) know the level of immunity provided by the state in question; 2) require the EDO to purchase insurance that covers the organization, volunteer board members, and staff.

The most important type of insurance from the board member's perspective is *director's and officer's liability insurance.* This is a specific type of insurance policy designed to cover any legal claims that might fall outside the volunteer immunity provided by applicable statutes. It is also important that the EDO have general liability insurance to cover injuries incurred by people in the EDO's facility or who participate in activities and events sponsored by the EDO.

EDO boards that sponsor community events might also consider purchasing event cancellation insurance to protect against claims that might result from the cancellation or postponement of a given event. Cancelling or postponing an event in which other organizations have an investment can lead to legal claims. Take the example of an EDO in a military community that sponsors a military appreciation day. In order to ensure maximum attendance, the EDO contracts with a big-name band to provide music. Then, just two days before the event is to take place, it must be cancelled or postponed. The band, which could have booked another event, might feel entitled to more than just the down payment made by the EDO to secure the booking.

This is just one example. I know of another in which a local EDO was sued when it cancelled the annual softball tournament it had sponsored for ten years. Most local companies fielded a team every year and the competition was intense. When the company that had held the title for several years was finally dethroned, its CEO vowed that his company would take the trophy back the following year. In the interim, the EDO's board decided that the competition to win the tournament was getting out of hand and doing more harm than good. The tournament had been conceived originally as a way to help local business leaders get to know each other and establish relationships from which they and the whole community might benefit.

Intended to generate good will among local businesses, over time the tournament had begun, instead, to create animosity. Consequently, the EDO's board voted to cancel the tournament. Claiming he had been "robbed" of an opportunity to reclaim what he called the "coveted tournament trophy," the CEO whose company had finally been dethroned in the previous year's tournament did something no one expected—he sued the EDO.

It can be difficult, even impossible, to predict how, when, or why a local EDO might become the target of a lawsuit. Consequently, it is important for volunteer board members to: 1) understand the extent of their immunity, and 2) ensure that the EDO purchases appropriate types of insurance with appropriate levels of coverage to protect against claims that might fall outside the coverage of volunteer immunity. The best advice for volunteer board members concerning immunity and insurance is this: seek the wise counsel of an attorney or an insurance agent with expertise and experience in the not-for-profit arena.

GENERAL RULES FOR EDO BOARD MEETINGS

Board meetings for local EDOs are typically conducted in accordance with well-defined protocols. What follows in this section are several general rules that will help ensure orderly board meetings and that will withstand any challenge that might be brought by a disgruntled stakeholder who tries to use a procedural argument to overturn a board decision.

Define a Quorum for Board Meetings

A quorum is the number of voting board members who must be present at a meeting in order for the board to take action (e.g. vote on motions, approve activities, accept recommendations, etc.). Typically a quorum is defined as being a simple majority of voting board members. However, the board itself decides how it will define a quorum. That definition then becomes part of the EDO's by-laws and must be strictly observed until such time as the board changes the by-laws; typically a procedure that requires more than one board meeting to achieve.

When defining a quorum, questions sometime arise concerning "proxy" voting and "electronic attendance." A board may choose to allow its members to send a proxy to meetings. A proxy is someone a voting member of the board sends in his or her place to be counted in the quorum and to vote on matters that come before the board. Boards that choose to allow proxy voting typically restrict how often this approach can be used. I recommend restricting proxy voting to avoid a situation in which board members send proxies more often than they attend themselves. Regardless of how your EDO's board chooses to handle proxy voting, the protocols should be recorded in the organization's by-laws.

Boards may also choose to allow voting members to attend meetings electronically—typically by speaker telephone. As with proxy voting, an electronic participant may be counted in the quorum provided the board makes the necessary provisions in its by-laws. Again, as with proxy voting, the practice of electronic attendance—if allowed—should be the exception rather than the rule.

Have a Meeting Agenda

Civic entrepreneurs who serve as volunteer board members for local EDOs tend to be successful, independent-minded people with strong opinions. Add to this that there are so many complex issues to deal with, so many competing interests to consider, and so many potential conflicts just waiting to erupt and you can see that EDO board meetings can be difficult to keep on track. The best way to ensure that you are able to conduct orderly board meetings that finish within a reasonable time frame is to always have a meeting agenda and some operating ground rules. Some rules of thumb about meeting agendas that you should be familiar with are:

■   The agenda should contain a starting time and a projected ending time.

■   All issues to be discussed during the meeting should be listed in the agenda along with the person responsible for each item. A typical agenda for an EDO board meeting would contain at least the following items: 1) review of the minutes of the previous meeting, 2) old business that still needs to be resolved, 3) new items of business to be dealt with, and 4) time and date of the next meeting.

■   All backup materials relating to agenda items should be attached to the minutes. Never waste the time of board members by interrupting a meeting to retrieve backup materials that could and should have been attached to the agenda.

■   The EDO's staff, acting on behalf of the board chair, should prepare and distribute the agenda and backup materials in accordance with the organization's by-laws. It is best to provide the agenda and backup materials 24 to 48 hours before the meeting. Any more and you might be cutting off items that need to be on the agenda. Any less and board members will have insufficient time to prepare for the meeting.

Keep Comprehensive Minutes of all Board Meetings

It is important to have an accurate record of what takes place in board meetings. As a member of a local EDO's board, you will want to make sure that a staff member is given the assignment of keeping minutes of meetings. By "keeping" minutes, I mean recording them during board meetings, distributing them after meetings, and maintaining a file of minutes for the record. It is best to have the same person record the minutes from meeting to meeting if this is possible.

There are two reasons for this: 1) consistency in style and composition are important, but difficult to achieve unless the same person records the minutes during each successive meeting; and 2) striking an appropriate balance between comprehensiveness and brevity is desirable, but achieving the desired balance takes practice and experience.

Action items—those decisions or assignments that require action on the part of a board member or staffer—should be recorded in such a way that they stand out from the text of the minutes and are easily seen (e.g. bold, italics, etc.). Such an approach will ensure that action items can be easily monitored until they have been completed.

Minutes should be distributed no more than 24 hours after a given meeting, and they should be kept on file for at least three years. Longer is better and forever is best. If questions, issues, or controversies arise concerning the EDO's actions, minutes are the board's official record. In addition, minutes are part of the history of the organization. They are an excellent source for helping the EDO remember its roots, retain its corporate memory, and maintain continuity over time.

Conduct Meetings According to Specific Rules of Order

There is a name for board meetings that are conducted without specific rules of order. That name is "chaos." Even without the controversies that often come up in board meetings, any gathering of bright, motivated, influential people determined to get things done will needs some rules of order to keep discussions on track and to prevent debates from getting out of hand.

Most boards simply adopt Roberts Rules of Order or a version of them as operating guidelines. Regardless of the specific system of rules adopted, the following essential elements should be understood by volunteer board members:

- *Motion.* Action is initiated by a motion made by a voting board member that begins as follows: "I move that we…" Any proposed action by the board should be initiated by a motion from a voting board member.

- *Second.* Before a motion is accepted for discussion, it must receive a second. This means that another board member deems the motion worthy of discussion. To second a motion so that it can be discussed simply say the word "second." Motions that fail to receive a second are said to "die for lack of a second." This brings up an important point. You do not have to agree with a motion in order to second it. Seconding a motion simply means that you want it to be discussed. You might second a motion so that you can speak against it in an attempt to defeat the motion. Without a second, a motion cannot be debated, discussed, or acted on in any way. Correspondingly, motions that are seconded may be discussed, voted on, amended, or tabled.

- *Discussion.* Once a motion has been seconded, board members are free to discuss it. You may speak in favor of the motion or against it, ask for clarification of the motion's intent, propose amendments, or recommend that the motion be tabled (i.e. put aside for action at a later date).

- *Amendments.* Discussion of a motion that has been seconded may reveal the need to: 1) ask for clarification of intent, 2) strengthen the language of the motion, or 3) correct an unintended misperception caused by the motion. The process for doing any of these things is called amending the motion and it works like this: 1) a voting board member proposes a change to the wording of the amendment, 2) the board chair or whomever is presiding asks the board members who made and seconded the motion if the proposed amendment is acceptable to them, and 3) if the board members who made and seconded the motion accept the amendment, the motion is acted on as amended (i.e. discussed further if necessary, voted on, or tabled).

- *Tabling.* During the discussion of a motion it will occasionally become apparent that more information is needed before the board can make an informed vote. When this situation arises, rather than risk taking insufficiently informed action or having the motion voted down because it is not fully understood, the board may choose to table it. Tabling a motion means putting it aside for the time being with the intention of bringing it up again at the next meeting of the board or at another specified time. The presiding officer or the person who made the motion may recommend that a motion be tabled. When a motion is tabled, a notation of the action is recorded in the minutes. The motion is then put on the agenda of the next board meeting— or another specified meeting—under "old business." During this meeting, the motion is reintroduced for discussion and appropriate action. It retains its second from the previous meeting.

- *Calling the question.* When it becomes apparent that an issue before the board has been sufficiently discussed and that any further discussion will be superfluous, a voting board member may call the question. By calling the question, a board member is saying, "We have discussed this issue long enough—let's vote." Calling the question is a strategy for keeping a meeting moving, not for avoiding discussion or cutting it off prematurely. Its best use is when discussion is becoming repetitive or redundant.

- *Voting.* Motions that are seconded may be amended or tabled as described earlier, but ultimately they must be put to the vote. Motions that receive a majority vote are approved. Those that fail to achieve a majority vote are disapproved. Votes on certain types of issues might require more than just a simple majority. When this is the case, the by-laws will so state. Voting is typically done in one of three ways depending on the EDO's by-laws: 1) simple voice vote, 2) show of hands, and 3) written ballot.

The various elements of order explained in this section really just scratch the surface of parliamentary procedure. They represent the bare minimum you will need to know to be an effective participant in board meetings. You can enhance the orderliness of board meetings by purchasing a copy of the book, Robert's Rules of Order, and studying the subject of parliamentary procedure in greater depth.

POTENTIAL LEGAL ISSUES AND THE EDO BOARD

Civic entrepreneurs who serve on the boards of local EDOs are often surprised to learn just how much responsibility they have accepted. Volunteer board members have fiduciary, ethical, anti-trust, and tax-related responsibilities in addition to their leadership and operational responsibilities. This section is included not to frighten, but to inform volunteer board members concerning their responsibilities. Serving on the board of a local EDO can be like navigating a ship—it's best to know where the rocks, shoals, and icebergs are located.

The rocks, shoals, and icebergs of EDO boards are several legal issues with which all board members should be familiar. These issues include federal tax compliance, anti-trust compliance, fiscal integrity, and apparent authority. These concepts are explained in the following paragraphs.

Federal Tax Compliance

If you are pulled over by a police officer for speeding, it will do you no good to say, "I didn't know the speed limit." The police officer will probably tell you that ignorance of the law is no excuse and, then, give you a ticket. The Internal Revenue Service (IRS) is like this police officer; it does not accept ignorance of the law as an excuse. Rather, it expects an EDO's board members to understand the board's responsibilities concerning federal taxes.

The board of a local EDO must ensure that: 1) the EDO properly submits its annual tax returns (typically the Form 990 or 990 EZ); and 2) the board's tax returns remain on file for at least three years, and are made available when properly asked for in accordance with public records requests procedures. Of course, the EDO's staff actually submits the Form 990/990 EZ and maintains the records, but the board is responsible for providing the oversight to ensure that this happens.

Anti-Trust Compliance

The boards of local EDOs typically consist of the community's most influential decision makers. Sometimes board members are from the same industry or business sector (e.g. banking, real estate, construction, manufacturing, defense contracting, etc.). When two or more decision makers have the ability to influence how business is conducted by making agreements that reduce or inhibit competition, the potential for anti-trust violations exists. The best way to guard against anti-trust charges arising from conversations with colleagues in the same business or industry sector is to simply avoid such conversations. Take a better-safe-than-sorry approach.

Fiscal Integrity

The board of a local EDO is responsible for ensuring the fiscal integrity of the organization. This does not mean that board members need to be CPAs. Rather, the best way to fulfill this obligation—even if you are a CPA—is to contract with a competent third party to provide an annual audit of the EDO's books. The EDO's staff will keep the books on a monthly basis and a volunteer board member will typically be named the organization's treasurer. The treasurer, working with the assigned staffer, will present the budget to the board at each successive board meeting throughout the year. Then, at the end of the fiscal year, a third-party audit will ensure that the EDO's books are in order.

Apparent Authority

Apparent authority is a legal concept that applies to the board's chair regardless of whether the position is called "board chair," "president," or any other title. A volunteer serving as board chair has specific authority as explained in the EDO's by-laws. An EDO's board chair is legally bound to not just exercise authority properly, but also to prevent other entities from usurping that authority. For example, the chair may not allow a committee or a task force to exercise authority it does not have. Allowing another entity to exercise authority it does not have amounts to granting it apparent authority.

STRATEGIC DIRECTION AND THE EDO BOARD

One of the key responsibilities of the EDO's board is to provide strategic direction for the organization. Providing strategic direction amounts to envisioning a desirable future for the community served by the EDO and developing a compelling picture of what that future will look like. The board's strategic direction should answer the following question: *From the perspective of economic development, where is the EDO trying to take this community?* The process by which the board answers this question is known as "strategic planning." The strategic planning process is covered later in this book. The purpose of this section is simply to make the point that providing strategic direction is an important responsibility of the EDO's board.

The most basic tool for communicating the board's strategic direction is the vision statement (which is developed as part of the strategic planning process). What follows is an example of a vision statement that could be used to convey a board's strategic direction for a local EDO:

> *Smithville will be a thriving community with a vibrant, diversified economy and high-wage employment opportunities for its citizens.*

This is a brief but compelling vision that provides clear strategic direction for the Smithville Economic Development Council (EDC). Although this vision consists of just one sentence, it communicates a powerful message. Consider the various elements of this vision:

- Thriving community
- Vibrant, diversified economy
- High-wage employment opportunities

In order for Smithville to become a "thriving community," its EDC will need to take the initiative in continually improving the community's economic base, business climate, and overall quality of life. In order for Smithville to have a "vibrant, diversified economy," its EDC will need to retain and expand existing businesses while simultaneously recruiting and home growing new businesses from several different sectors. In order for Smithville to have "high-wage employment opportunities," its EDC will need to do more than just create jobs, it will have to create well-paying jobs in organizations that offer competitive benefits and opportunities for advancement. Providing strategic direction for local EDOs is a key responsibility of volunteer boards. Developing a comprehensive vision statement is the most important tool for providing strategic direction.

LEADERSHIP AND THE EDO BOARD

Providing leadership for the EDO and the community is one of the most important responsibilities of the volunteer board member. There are a number of different definitions of leadership, but in the current context the concept means:

> *The ability to inspire people who may have different agendas to fully cooperate in pursuing a strategic direction for economic development that is in the long-term best interests of the community.*

The characteristics of leaders who are able to do what this definition says include at least the following:

- Positive role model
- Persuasive
- Balanced commitment to economic growth and quality of life
- Good communication skills
- Consensus builder
- Participative

The good news is that these characteristics of a good leader also apply to civic entrepreneurs. Most civic entrepreneurs are positive role models, persuasive, have a balanced commitment to economic growth and quality of life, good communication skills, and the ability to build consensus among disparate groups and individuals with different agendas.

Positive Role Model

If you are going to expect others community leaders to put aside their personal interests in favor of what is best for the community, you have to set a consistent example of doing so yourself. The *do-as-I-say-not-as-I-do* approach will not work for leaders in economic development. In any community, there are so many different and often competing interests that a poor or inconsistent example on the part of a volunteer board member can become an excuse others use for refusing to put aside personal interest and support projects that are in the best interests of the community.

Persuasive

The ability to persuade is a critical leadership characteristic for volunteer board members. This is because people cannot always be counted on to do the right thing just because it is the right thing. Rather, people are prone to make decisions and form opinions based on what is sometimes called enlightened self-interest. This is where persuasion comes in. In order to bring all of the right people to the table and begin the process of consensus building, you will have to be persuasive. Often you will have to paint a vivid "word picture" of your vision for economic development and explain it to others in terms they can understand. In other words, you will have to personalize the message by explaining how, in the long run, THEY and the community will benefit from the project in question.

Balanced Commitment

Done properly, economic development will simultaneously improve the community's economy and enhance its quality of life. When this happens, there is an appropriate balance between economic development and the quality of life. However, there is an ever-present tendency for economic development to get out of balance, and the tendency applies in both directions. Poorly managed growth and development can rob a community of the very attributes that make it a desirable location in the first place. This is the old *eating-your-seed-corn* error applied to economic development. On the other hand, a community can become so restrictive in its zoning, permitting, and support of economic development that attempts to improve the economy and create new jobs are continually squeezed to death by a constrictive, python-like bureaucracy. This is why it so important for volunteer board members to maintain an appropriately balanced commitment to both economic development and quality of life concerns.

The difference between well-managed economic development and uncontrolled economic growth is like the difference between a well-tended rose garden and an infestation of kudzu. As a volunteer board member in a local EDO, part of your responsibility is to ensure well-managed economic development. Civic entrepreneurs who allow community growth to become the economic development equivalent of a kudzu infestation are failing in the leadership aspect of their responsibilities.

Good Communication Skills

Good leaders are good communicators—they have to be. People will not follow someone who fails to keep them informed, will not listen, or is unable to articulate a coherent sense of direction. Communication is an essential leadership skill because people will not trust someone who fails to communicate, and they will not follow someone they do not trust. Verbal, non-verbal, and written communication skills are all important, but listening skills are essential. Good leaders must be good listeners.

When interacting with others about economic development, remember to apply the following effective listening strategies:

- Look the speaker in the eye and give him your undivided attention.

- Concentrate on what is being said and do not interrupt.

- Do not allow yourself to be put off by anger or frustration on the part of the speaker. Concentrate on the real message behind the anger and frustration.

- Once the speaker has stated her case, ask any questions that are necessary for clarification or to gain more complete information.

- Conclude the conversation by paraphrasing and repeating back what you think the speaker has told you.

- Keep yourself in "neutral" non-verbally (e.g. do not send non-verbal signals of disagreement, impatience, anger, boredom, fear, etc.). Maintain a facial expression that says: "I am listening and care about what you have to say."

Consensus Builder

Good leaders are good consensus builders. One definition of a good leader is someone who can convince others to go where they are not yet ready to go. Because economic development, by its very nature means change and people tend to resist change, civic entrepreneurs must be good at persuading people to overcome human nature and support the changes that are a part of well-managed economic development.

Convincing people with different agendas, perspectives, goals, and ambitions to work together for the greater good requires building consensus around the concept of change. Building consensus requires that civic entrepreneurs be willing to push, pull, or back off as needed and to know when each approach is appropriate. The keys to building consensus for economic development initiatives are vision, commitment, communication, patience, and persistence.

Participative

The best leaders in an economic development setting take a participative approach. This means they are non-directive and inclusive in their dealings with people. This is important because the people who have a stake in economic development cannot be simply ordered to do their part or to go along with initiatives the EDO would like to undertake. This is another reason why leaders of EDOs must be good consensus builders.

When participative leaders have to make a decision, they identify everyone with a stake in the decision—people who will be affected by the decision or will play a role in carrying it out—and find ways to involve them in the decision-making process. In other words, participative leaders give stakeholders in economic development a voice in the process.

Critics of participative leadership claim that it is too time consuming and that it slows down the economic development process. This criticism is sometimes well-founded. However, more often than not economic development is better served when it follows the slow-but-steady example of the proverbial tortoise rather than the full-speed-ahead example of the hare.

Civic entrepreneurs who exclude stakeholders during the formative stages of an economic development initiative are likely to run into unexpected opposition at inopportune times. For example, I know of a case in which failing to include stakeholders in the developmental stages of an economic development project led to an unfortunate situation in which an important prospect was met at the airport by a line of protestors telling him to go else where—which he did.

I learned about the value of participative leadership in an instructive way while serving in the U.S. Marine Corps. I was playing for one of the Marine Corps' football teams during the last months of my enlistment. The game was tied six to six with just four seconds left to play. My team was on the opponent's one-yard line. That was the good news. The bad news was that we didn't have a field goal kicker; a fact that accounted for the tied score.

Our opponent had scored two field goals. We had scored a touchdown, but missed the extra point—by a mile. Our only way to win the game was to put the ball in the end zone. Victory was just one yard away, but after enduring a brutal defensive battle all afternoon, that one yard looked like a mile. That's when something happened I had never seen or even heard of in the Marine Corps. Our coach called a timeout and motioned our entire offense to join him on the sideline.

Then, he surprised us my saying: "Men, I have to call the only play we have left in this game. We either win or lose on this call. Before I decide what play to call, I want to hear your opinions. You are closer to this than I am. You line up across from your opponent on every play. You know better than I do who on the other team is tired, who is dogging it, and where they might be vulnerable." For our coach, a grizzled Gunnery Sergeant who typically said very little and didn't need to, this was a long speech. Even more surprising was that he had asked our opinion. This "Gunny" was definitely old Corps. His attitude toward our opinions usually went like this: "If I want you to have an opinion I'll give you one."

When we had recovered sufficiently from the shock of the Gunny asking for our opinions, an offensive lineman said: "Coach, the defensive tackle across from me is their best lineman, but he is out on his feet. He's been going both ways all day and can hardly stand up. In fact, between plays, he stays down on his knees trying to catch his breath." When no one else offered a better observation, the Gunny simply nodded and then called a play that ran the ball right at the other team's tired out defensive tackle. The play worked. Our fullback ran through the hole created by double-teaming the opposing defensive tackle and into the end zone standing up.

The Gunny did not ask us to make the decision for him concerning which play to call. He just asked for our observations so that he could make a more informed decision. This is what participative leaders do and, in economic development, it is the best approach. Yes, this approach can cause initiatives to move more slowly than you might like, and yes it can give opponents of economic development a soap box from which to voice their opposition. On the other hand, it can give you a chance to detect potential opposition early in the process, and take steps to deal with it.

Chapter Three

::

THE LOCAL ECONOMIC DEVELOPMENT ORGANIZATION (EDO)

CHAPTER OUTLINE

- Criteria for success
- Mission of the local EDO
- Organizational structure
- By-laws
- Board of directors
- Budget and finance
- Committees
- Programs
- Accreditation

What should a local EDO look like? How should an EDO function? How do we know if our EDO is functioning as well as it should be? These are the types of questions volunteer leaders of local EDO's should ask and often do. One of the key responsibilities of volunteer leaders is to be good stewards of the funding invested in their EDO. This means that you—as a volunteer leader—are responsible for maximizing the efficiency and effectiveness of the EDO. This chapter provides the information volunteers leaders need to know to ensure that their EDO is structured for success and is working as well as it should be.

CRITERIA FOR SUCCESS

Local EDOs are like businesses in that we know what it takes for them to succeed. This section explains several criteria that can be used to determine if a local EDO is structured for success. These same criteria can be used to help pin point the reasons why a struggling EDO is not performing at the desired level.

Knowledgeable, Committed Volunteer Leadership

The most important factor in the success of a local EDO is the quality of the volunteers who serve in leadership positions such as board members, officers, committee chairs, task force leaders, team captains, and event coordinators. Individuals in these positions need to be knowledgeable of economic development and committed to it. Being a successful decision-maker and leader in another field is important because decision-making and leadership skills are transferable. However, even the most knowledgeable, committed professional in another field may know little or nothing about economic development.

As a leader in your local EDO, you need to be knowledgeable of the basics of economic development and committed to applying them in ways that serve the best interests of your community. The purpose of this book is to help you learn the basics of economic development and how you can apply them in ways that will help your EDO achieve its mission.

Clearly Stated Mission that is Understood by all Stakeholders

Every organization has a mission—a reason for being, a purpose. A clearly stated mission will describe precisely what an organization exists to do. A well-conceived mission statement will help keep the EDO's volunteers and professionals properly focused. A local EDO should have a mission statement that is understood by all stakeholders including volunteer board members, officers, staff members, funding agencies, and the general public. Most EDOs build their mission statement around the concept of job creation or enhancing the community's economy. Developing a mission statement for your local EDO is covered in more depth as part of the strategic planning process in Chapter 5.

Sufficient Funding

Economic development is like most endeavors in that you get what you pay for. Money will not overcome poor leadership, poor management, or other systemic shortcomings, but, on the other hand, even the best led and best managed organization will be limited by insufficient funding. Some local EDOs are funded solely by private dollars while others receive public funding, typically in the form of a local government appropriation. However, the trend is toward public-private partnerships in which funding comes from both private and government sources.

Appropriate Organizational Structure

It is important that local EDOs—like all organizations—be structured for success. The organization should be structured to efficiently and effectively carry out it mission. Sometimes local EDOs are structured as they are because of tradition, personnel quirks, or leadership whims. In such cases, the organization rarely achieves its full potential.

Structuring a local EDO for success means that the organizational structure should mirror the mission statement. For example, if a local EDO's mission statement emphasizes retention, expansion, local start-ups, and recruiting, its organizational structure should reflect these priorities. This probably sounds like a statement of the obvious, and it should. However, I have worked as a consultant with several EDOs that had yawning gaps between their stated missions and their organizational structure. For example, one EDO I worked with stated in its mission that its number one priority was retention and expansion of existing companies. However, the organization was structured for just one activity: recruiting.

If this EDO's number one priority was really retention and expansion of existing businesses, some portion of the organization' staff should have been dedicated to those priorities. There should have been an on-going retention and expansion program built into the EDO's organizational structure so that time, effort, and expertise could be invested in these worthy pursuits. Unfortunately, this was not the case. One hundred percent of the EDO's budget and expertise were dedicated to recruiting; a fact that eventually caused major problems when existing businesses began to complain about their membership dues being used for no purpose other than recruiting.

Professional Practitioners

One of the most important duties of a local EDO's board is hiring a competent economic development professional as the organization's CEO. This individual is responsible for hiring, supervising, and developing a competent staff; carrying out the policies of the organization's board; implementing the EDO's strategic plan; managing day-to-day operations; developing, implementing, and monitoring specific programs; and representing the EDO in the community as well as with funding providers. Hiring the right economic development professional as the organization's CEO is critical. Chapter 4 is dedicated to covering this important topic in greater detail.

Competent Support Personnel

Economic development is business. Consequently, a local EDO should be run like a business. Those who fund the organization expect efficiency, effectiveness, and professionalism. This means that competent individuals with the proper training and experience are needed in all staff positions. Staff personnel tend to the details of the EDO's daily operations. The better they do their jobs, the better the organization functions.

Supportive Community

Even the best led, best managed, best funded EDO will struggle without the support of the community it serves. A community must want economic development in order for the process to succeed in the long run. An EDO that serves an anti-economic development community will always be hampered in its efforts. This is because those who oppose economic development can usually find ways to throw up roadblocks. Their tactics typically include lobbying against the EDO's public funding, writing letters to the editor, making their opposition known to prospects, and organizing citizen committees to apply political pressure in opposition to economic development.

In any community, there are almost always those who oppose economic development. However, if such people are in the minority—even if they are a vocal minority—economic development can be a viable enterprise. It is when those opposed to economic development are in the majority that the concept ceases to be viable.

This is why establishing and maintaining community support is such an important responsibility of the local EDO's volunteer leaders. Within their own businesses, in civic clubs, at social functions, in political forums, and wherever else people in the community congregate, you and your fellow volunteers should work to build support for economic development.

MISSION OF THE LOCAL EDO

The importance of a clearly articulated mission statement was emphasized in the previous section. This section goes into the subject of the mission of the local EDO in more depth and detail. The way a local EDO is structured, funded, and operated should be driven by its mission. The mission statement for a local EDO should define the organization, describe its service area, and list its primary functions. When developing a new mission statement for a local EDO or when revising an existing mission statement, make sure it answers the following questions:

■   What is the overall purpose of the organization?

■   What are the principle functions of the organization?

■   What is the geographic area served by the organization?

PURPOSE OF THE LOCAL EDO

A local EDO is in business to continually improve the economy of its community and to create good jobs for people in that community. EDOs exist to create jobs, diversify and strengthen the local economy, and undertake other related activities. Consequently, the first element in an EDO's mission statement will typically mention improving the local economy, creating jobs, and/or diversifying the local economy. As a volunteer leader, it is important to keep the EDO focused on these fundamental purposes. Your EDO may choose to serve other purposes, but these other purposes should not be allowed to inhibit the organization's ability to fulfill its core purposes.

Principal Functions of the Local EDO

Most EDOs commit to the following functions, although different EDOs will prioritize these functions differently:

■   Retention of existing businesses

■   Expansion of existing businesses

■   Start-up of new businesses (entrepreneurship)

■   Recruitment of businesses from other locations (business attraction)

Retention of existing businesses must be a high priority in local EDOs. There are two reasons for this. The first is that the EDO's dues-paying members are existing businesses, as are potential new members. EDOs that collect membership dues from local businesses and then ignore their needs while focusing solely on business attraction deserve the criticism they are sure to receive. The second reason is the damage done to a community's morale, economy, and image when a business closes its doors and goes out of business or, worse yet, relocates to another more support-ive community.

When a business closes down or relocates, people who are accustomed to being gainfully employed, tax-paying citizens suddenly find them-selves out of work—a frightening prospect for anyone. The fear, frustra-tion, and bitterness they experience can create a ripple effect that spreads throughout the community causing morale problems; even among those who still have jobs. A "who-is-next" mentality can set in.

Economic problems invariably follow in the wake of a business clos-ing or relocation as the process associated with job growth goes into reverse. When this happens, the positives generated by increased spend-ing are replaced by the negatives that result from restricted spending. Depending on the number of jobs lost, a once vibrant service sector can stagnate or even decline. Bills that in previous months were paid on time begin to show up as delinquent. Eventually, if the jobs are not replaced, the community's tax rolls begin to suffer and public services, once taken for granted, are cut back or even eliminated. This snowballing of eco-nomic negatives can cause a community's morale to plummet.

Business closings and relocations can also damage a community's im-age—both its self-image and its external image. As is the case in most endeavors, in economic development, success breeds success and failure breeds failure. Losing a major employer can have the same counterpro-ductive effect on a community that losing a major competition some-times has on a sports team. It can take away the community's positive momentum and replace it with self doubt. Self doubt can devolve into a negative self-image that is difficult for the community to overcome.

In addition to problems with the community's self image, there is the problem of how prospects and relocation consultants might view a community that has lost a major employer. Prospects would be remiss if they failed to ask "why?" This does not mean that losing a company will automatically prevent the community from attracting others. In fact, sometimes a business closing will actually turn out to be a positive when a prospect views it as an opportunity to acquire a ready-made workforce and a fully-functioning facility. However, you should bear in mind that it is easier to get prospects to view things in this way if the business in question went out of business than if it relocated because the community failed to support it. The point to remember here is that retention of existing businesses must be a high priority of a local EDO.

Expansion of existing businesses should also be a high priority for local EDOs. When an existing business expands, a community reaps all of the benefits associated with attracting a new company or starting up a new business without some of the potential negatives. The EDO saves the costs associated with recruiting, and the community experiences less impact on its infrastructure. It costs local government agencies less to extend existing sewer, water, and road systems than it does to construct the new ones that are often required to accommodate new businesses that must develop new parcels of land and build facilities.

Assisting in the start-up of new businesses from within the community often gets less attention than it should in local EDOs. In every community there are people who want to turn their ideas into businesses. When this happens and the business created succeeds, jobs are created. Since job creation is a fundamental purpose of economic development, business entrepreneurs and EDOs are natural allies. Chapter 9 explains what EDOs can do to promote entrepreneurship in the communities they serve.

Attracting businesses (recruiting) from other locations is a high priority in most EDOs and the highest in many. Even when local EDOs claim that retention and expansion of existing businesses are their highest priorities, they often put more effort into recruiting. The reason for this is what I call the *home-run syndrome*. If economic development were baseball, retention would equate to hitting a single. Expansion is like hitting a double, and a new start-up is like hitting a triple. But attracting a new business from another community is like hitting a home run; at least in the minds of many stakeholders.

Attracting a new company from out of town is a glitzy, high profile, media worthy event. Few things in economic development will get the attention of the press, electronic media, and politicians faster than a major recruiting success. In fact, I have seen communities turn the relocation of a small company that provides relatively few new jobs into a major event while ignoring local businesses that have quietly but steadily expanded over the years thereby creating many more jobs than the new company did or ever will. As a member of your local EDO's board, you will want to caution your colleagues against falling prey to the home-run syndrome.

GEOGRAPHIC SERVICE AREA

Local EDO's typically have well-defined geographic service areas. The service area for a local EDO might be a county, municipality, region, or a combination of these. Typically, a denser population will result in a smaller service area. The obverse is typically also true. A sparser population will result in a larger service area. Because of local exigencies, this rule of thumb does not always apply, but it usually holds true. Regardless of the actual size of an EDO's service area, it should be well-defined and included in the organization's mission statement.

SAMPLE MISSION STATEMENTS

A mission statement for a local EDO should contain the following elements: 1) a statement of the organization's purpose, 2) an explanation of the organization's principal functions, and 3) a description of the organization's service area. In addition to containing these three elements, a well-written mission statement will have the following characteristics:

- Brief, but comprehensive
- Simply written and easily understood
- Oriented toward "what" rather than "how"

The three mission statements for local EDOs that follow are provided as examples that meet these three criteria:

The mission of the Morris County Economic Development Council is to create jobs that add depth and diversity to the County's economy. Principal functions are retention and expansion of existing businesses, start-up of new businesses, and recruitment of businesses from other locations.

The mission of the Pike-Monroe Economic Development Council is to continually improve the economy of Pike and Monroe Counties. The EDC's principal functions are business retention, expansion, recruiting, and start-ups.

The mission of the economic development division of the Analton County Chamber of Commerce is job creation and diversification of the community's economic base. Principal functions are retention, expansion, start-ups, and recruitment of business, industry, and government employers to the greater Analton region.

ORGANIZATIONAL STRUCTURE

There is no organizational structure for an EDO that will guarantee success in economic development. However, I have developed a simple equation that can be helpful when deciding how to structure local EDOs for optimum results:

Consideration +Accommodation = Optimization

In this equation, "consideration" refers to consideration of the needs, strengths, weaknesses, and exigencies of the local community. "Accommodation" refers to making sure the structure chosen accommodates the EDO's mission. Remember, the organizational structure must enable the EDO to effectively carry out its mission. "Optimization" means that local EDOs can arrive at the optimum organizational structure by carefully *considering* local exigencies and properly *accommodating* the organization's mission.

The organizational structure of a local EDO is influenced by the following factors: governance, management, operations, and funding. The most successful local EDOs satisfy the governance, management, and operational factors by having the following: 1) a board of directors comprised of volunteer community leaders—civic entrepreneurs—who establish policy, provide leadership, set the strategic direction, and help secure an appropriate level of funding; 2) an economic development professional to manage the organization, implement board policy, and carry out the EDO's strategic plan; and 3) a competent support staff to handle the daily operations of the EDO.

There are three widely-used options for securing the funds needed to operate a local EDO: 1) private funding including membership dues, 2) public funding from local government sources, and 3) public-private funding. The relative advantages and disadvantages of these approaches are explained in the sections that follow.

Private Funding

With this approach, the organization receives its funding solely from private-sector sources; typically in the form of membership dues. This approach has advantages and disadvantages. The main advantages are *confidentiality* and *autonomy*. Confidentiality in the current context means that the EDO can work with prospects without making the proceedings public. This can be an important advantage. Prospects demand confidentiality when working with the various communities on their list of possible relocation sites. In fact, few things will undermine a relocation deal faster than premature publicity.

Autonomy in the current context means that the EDO's board can set its own course for the organization without the complications of politics. Privately funded EDOs are typically better able to make decisions based on business rather than political considerations. For example, elected officials who are running for office are sometimes inclined to pressure EDOs to pursue less worthy projects in order to show the voters that they—the politicians—have helped create new jobs for their constituents.

The disadvantages of the private-funding approach are *distractions* and *disparate influence*. With only private sources of funding to depend on, a local EDO's budget can be tenuous and unpredictable. For example, memberships sold one year must be re-sold the next year and the next and the next in order to just stay even. This is the concept of member retention, a worthy but time-consuming and unpredictable endeavor. As a result, the staff of a privately-funded EDO can find itself investing more time in trying to maintain a viable budget than in undertaking economic development initiatives. This is like the tennis player who spends the entire match focusing on the scoreboard rather than the game—not a good strategy.

Many privately-funded EDOs adopt a graduated dues structure based on the principle that the higher the dues paid, the greater the privilege of membership. In other words, an organization that chooses to pay a higher level of dues receives more benefits from the EDO. For example, one EDO I have worked with has a "pay to play" policy that allows any organization to have a seat on the board if it is willing to pay the price of three times the highest level of membership dues.

This can be an excellent way to enhance the EDO's budget, but it can also lead to the second disadvantage of private funding: disparate influence. This disadvantage occurs when a small number of members account for a large percentage of the EDO's budget. This financial dependency gives a minority of board members more influence than the single vote they can cast on issues that come before the EDO's board. If one of these more influential members of the board opposes a given initiative, there is always the threat, even if unstated, that it might resign from the EDO and take its funding with it. This is the concept of disparate influence.

Used in the current context, disparate influence means that certain members, because they pay higher dues, tend to have more influence than other members in spite of the one-board-member-one-vote rule adopted in most EDOs. Where this can become a major problem is when an influential member of the EDO uses his or her power to pressure the board to make decisions that serve a specific agenda rather than the overall community.

Maintaining an adequate budget from year to year can be a challenge in privately-funded EDOs, but growing the budget can be even more difficult. This is because the best method available for growing the budget is continually attracting new members. This is the concept of new member recruiting. There is an inherent problem that can make new member recruiting a difficult challenge.

There are only so many businesses that are realistic candidates for membership in the EDO. A realistic candidate for membership is one that meets the following criteria: 1) stands to benefit as an organization from its involvement, and 2) has executive-level managers who will commit the time necessary to be effective participants. The number of candidates in any community that meet these criteria will always be limited—even in larger communities.

Public Funding

With this approach, all funding comes from governmental appropriations, typically provided by counties, cities, or a combination of these. A publicly-funded EDO is often, though not always, a department within a local government agency such as a county, city, or other municipality. In such cases, the EDO's policy and strategic direction are established by local elected officials (e.g. members of the county commission, city council, etc.). The EDO's manager and staff are typically employees of the government agency in question, and the manager reports to a public official such as a county manager, city manager, or mayor.

Less frequently, publicly-funded EDOs are organized in the same manner as privately-funded EDOs. They have a board of directors consisting of volunteer community leaders, an economic development professional who manages the organization, and a staff of paid employees. Such organizations are typically established as a 501(c)6 corporation in terms of their legal structure. The only difference is that the organization receives its funding from a government entity such as a county commission or city council rather than from dues paid by private members. This approach to funding local EDOs is not widely used, but when it is the community served is usually rural. Sparsely populated communities often have such a limited business base that exclusively private funding is not a feasible option. In such communities, rather than add an economic development department to county or city government, elected officials choose to fund a 501(c)6 organization as the less expensive option.

The public funding approach has the advantage of providing a fairly predictable funding base and being broadly representative since local elected officials typically represent all segments of the community. On the other hand, there are disadvantages with this approach. The first is that governmental agencies are subject to fluctuations in tax revenue for a variety of reasons such as cuts in the millage rate and economic downturns. When governmental agencies are forced to absorb funding reductions, economic development is always a tempting target for budget cuts.

The second disadvantage of public funding is that it can become a political football during the government agency's annual budget deliberations; and with economic development it often does. In any community there will be those who oppose economic development, even in communities that are generally supportive of the concept. Local government budget deliberations are conducted as public forums. Public forums give naysayers—even though they may be a minority—opportunities to publicly voice their opposition. This can become a problem because some of the best, most important economic development projects can be controversial. This is a fact of life in economic development; one that all involved should understand.

Overcoming the opposition of nay-sayers, winning and maintaining the support of politicians, and dealing with an array of other issues that inevitably surface when undertaking economic development initiatives require commitment, perseverance, creativity, and the various other attributes of the entrepreneur. Consequently, EDOs that receive public funding must be led by civic entrepreneurs who have these attributes, know how to use them, and are willing to do so.

Public-Private Funding

Public-private partnerships have become a widely used approach for funding local EDOs. The reasons for the popularity of this approach are the advantages it can offer. One of the principle advantages is the ability to spread the costs of economic development among both public and private funding sources. By pooling their resources, public agencies and private businesses can increase a community's overall investment in economic development while minimizing their individual costs. Another advantage is that public-private partnerships accommodate the fact that most economic development initiatives require the involvement of both public officials and private community leaders.

For example, when working with a prospect, private sector representatives of a local EDO can speak with authority concerning what it is like to do business in the community. In addition, they are likely to have more credibility with prospects than will public officials or economic development practitioners. Public sector representatives, on the other hand, can speak with authority on such issues as taxes, education, permitting, environmental regulations, zoning, and infrastructure improvements.

Perhaps the most important benefit of the public-private approach to funding local EDOs is that it tends to incorporate the advantages of the other approaches while mitigating the disadvantages. It provides the more stable funding base associated with public appropriations, but with augmentation from private membership dues. In addition, it involves public officials first hand in economic development initiatives without giving up the autonomy enjoyed by privately funded EDOs.

Local EDOs that are public-private partnerships and that establish a 501(c)6 legal structure are able to protect the proprietary information of prospects in the same way as privately funded EDOs. Public-private funding also tends to balance the influence of individual board members from both sectors. In fact, EDOs that receive public and private funds typically try to maintain an approved ratio to ensure a balance in the influence of the two sectors. A widely adopted ratio is 50 percent private and 50 percent public, although ratios can vary widely depending on local exigencies. An should always err on the side of private members.

The public-private partnership is an excellent model for local EDOs, but it is not perfect. No model is. As with any partnership, a public-private EDO will occasionally experience tension between the partners. In any discussion of economic development initiatives, public and private members of the EDO's board are likely to bring different perspectives to the table. Disagreements are common in such cases and to be expected. Consequently, it is essential that volunteer leaders of local EDOs learn how to compromise on strategy without compromising on principle and to disagree without being disagreeable.

Local elected officials on the EDO's board should be cognizant of the natural tension that exists in any partnership, and prepared to take appropriate steps to deal with it in a positive manner. Team building and mediation training for board members can be helpful, as can less formal activities that help board members from both sectors get to know each other better as people and colleagues.

Stand-Alone Not-for-Profit or Affiliate Organization?

The final consideration concerning organizational structure is whether to establish the EDO as a stand-alone not-for-profit corporation or as an affiliate of an existing organization such as a chamber of commerce. Both approaches have advantages and disadvantages. Structuring the EDO as a stand-alone organization requires legal incorporation which can be complex and expensive. On the other hand, stand-alone organizations are able to focus on their mission without fear of running afoul of the affiliate organization, being overshadowed by it, or being confused with it in the minds of stakeholders.

Structuring the local EDO as an affiliate allows it to operate under the auspices of an existing not-for-profit organization. This eliminates the trouble and expense of incorporation, and can save on fixed overhead costs if these costs can be shared with the parent organization. On the other hand, this approach can subject the EDO to the *step-child syndrome* in which the needs and mission of the parent organization take precedence over those of the EDO.

Another perspective on this issue is having separate business-development organizations operating in the same community such as a stand-alone EDO and a chamber of commerce. This situation can lead to counterproductive turf battles if not handled properly. In communities with a stand-alone EDO and a chamber of commerce, coordination and cooperation between the two organizations is essential, even to the point of sharing board members.

If you serve on the board of a stand-alone EDO in a community that also has a chamber of commerce, you can help promote cooperation if you understand the differences between the organizations. These differences include the following: 1) chambers of commerce tend to attract more of their members from the service sector (e.g. retail, residential real estate, banking, hospitality, attorneys, healthcare, etc.) while EDOs attract more of their members from engineering, manufacturing, commercial development, defense contracting, processing, etc.); 2) chambers of commerce tend to provide more opportunities for their members to network to help them market their products and services to each other (relationships marketing) while EDOs focus more on business expansion, business attraction, and new business start-ups; and 3) chambers of commerce typically focus more on community development while EDOs focus more on economic development.

Often the differences between chambers of commerce and EDOs are more a matter of emphasis than absolutes. Chambers emphasize the service sector and networking, but they welcome members from other sectors and will sometimes get involved in helping recruit new businesses to their communities. EDOs emphasize the manufacturing, processing, and technology sectors, but they also welcome banks and other service providers as members and will occasionally offer networking opportunities for their members. In communities that have an active, forward-looking EDO and an equally assertive chamber of commerce, it is a good idea to establish at least informal protocols for mutual support.

BY-LAWS

The by-laws of a local EDO are the rules that govern the organization's everyday operation. A well-written set of by-laws achieves an appropriate balance between being restrictive on one hand and flexible on the other. By-laws need to be restrictive enough to provide clear, unambiguous direction, but flexible enough to give the organization room to maneuver. By-laws that are too restrictive will tie the hands of decision makers. On the other hand, by-laws that are too flexible will lose their meaning. Achieving an appropriate balance between these two key characteristics is the goal.

The actual contents of the by-laws for a given EDO will vary depending on the exigencies of the community served and the type of legal structure the EDO adopts. Typically, a local EDO will have at least the following sections in its by-laws:

- Section I: Organization's name
- Section II: Organization's location(s)
- Section III: Purpose
- Section IV: Members and meetings
- Section V: Board of directors
- Section VI: Officers
- Section VII: Executive committee
- Section VIII: Committee structure
- Section IX: Finances
- Section X: Indemnification
- Section XI: Amending the by-laws
- Section XII: Periodic review

This is just one example of a typical structure for the by-laws of a local EDO. Format, content, and sequence can vary from organization to organization. This is one of those areas in which the EDO's leadership is well-advised to seek qualified legal assistance. In some states, the incorporation process specifies what must be contained in the by-laws of a not-for-profit corporation while in other states the process simply requires that there be by-laws.

A well-written set of by-laws can prevent counter-productive squabbling among board members over procedural issues. However, there is one important caution about by-laws I always give to volunteer leaders of local EDOs: *If you have by-laws, follow them. If the by-laws are unsound, revise them but do not ignore or violate them.* Boards that ignore their own by-laws run the risk of having their actions challenged and even over-ruled on procedural grounds. Board decisions that are made in accordance with the EDO's by-laws are usually on firmer ground legally and procedurally than those that violate them.

I stress the importance of following your EDO's by-laws because it has been my experience that boards sometimes get into the habit of ignoring their by-laws out of convenience or neglect. After all, reviewing by-laws can make for some boring reading. Ignoring the EDO's by-laws may not be a problem until a situation arises where someone is unhappy with a decision of the board and decides to challenge it on either legal or procedural grounds, or both. When this happens, the EDO's by-laws suddenly take on a new level of importance. Consequently, the best advice I can give volunteers concerning by-laws is to have them, know them, and follow them.

BOARD OF DIRECTORS

A local EDO's board is its most important component. Volunteer board members set the tone for the organization. They provide leadership, strategic direction, fiscal oversight, financial support, and community linkages. They also hire and fire the CEO. These are all important responsibilities that must be undertaken with wisdom and commitment if the EDO is to be successful. I you serve on your EDO's board or would like to, this section is about you: who you are, what you do, how you are selected, how long you serve, and how you can be removed from the board if necessary.

Responsibilities of Board Members

The primary responsibilities of the board and its members are as follows: 1) providing leadership, 2) establishing strategic direction, 3) developing policy, 4) hiring and firing the CEO, 5) helping secure financial support, 6) providing fiscal oversight, and 7) linking the organization to the community. Board members will also be called on to assist in hosting visiting prospects, help identify potential prospects, and perform other miscellaneous duties that require the special assets they bring to the table.

Board Composition and Size

When initially establishing a board for a local EDO or when examining the viability of an existing board, the following questions are pertinent: 1) How big is big enough? 2) How big is too big? 3) How small is too small? and 4) Who should be on the board? There is no magic number for establishing the size of an EDO's board. The optimum sized board is large enough to be broadly representative of the EDO's various constituencies, but small enough to be responsive when conducting business.

A small board is usually better able to respond to opportunities in a timely manner while a large board is usually more diverse and broadly representative of the community. A compromise approach used by EDOs in handling the small-versus-large issue is to have a comprehensive, diverse policy board (large) that meets only quarterly or every other month and an executive board (small) that meets more frequently. The smaller board is empowered to act on behalf of the larger board on a well-defined list of issues and in unusual circumstances.

The question of who should serve on the board of the local EDO is often asked? The best candidates for board positions meet the following criteria: 1) can benefit from their involvement, 2) will commit the time necessary to be effective, 3) have influence in the community, and 4) are a key decision maker in their own organization. These criteria apply to all potential board members regardless of their respective professional fields.

In addition to securing board members who meet these criteria, it is important to have representatives from several specific fields in the private and public sectors. In other words, it is a good idea to ensure that certain fields are represented on the local EDO's board. From the public sector EDOs can benefit from the participation of county commissioners, county managers, city council members, city managers, mayors, planning and zoning professionals, property appraisers, tax collectors, educators (k-12 and higher education), and representatives of public utilities.

From the private sector, local EDOs can benefit from the participation of business leaders from such fields as banking, investment brokering, utilities, telecommunications, manufacturing, transportation, law, accounting, real estate, small business, real estate development, processing, distribution, the media, construction, engineering, architecture, and medicine.

Terms of Office

How long should a board member's term of office last? How many terms in office should a board member be allowed to serve? These questions should be answered in the EDO's by-laws, but not before careful consideration has been given to the issue of balance. The concept of balance in the current context refers to the balance that should exist on the EDO's board between new and experienced members. New board members bring fresh ideas and new perspectives to the table. Experienced board members balance these attributes with depth of knowledge and corporate memory. The best boards are those that achieve an appropriate balance between new and experienced members.

This desirable balance can be achieved by assigning staggered terms of office. Selected members can serve one, two, or three year terms. In this way, a certain number of members turn over every year. This has the salutary effect of bringing in new ideas while still retaining the corporate memory. Experience shows that a turnover of less than 25 percent per year is too little and more than 50 percent is too much. However, a caveat is in order here. This level of turnover can be difficult or even impossible to achieve in small communities. When this is the case, a common sense application of the turn over concept can achieve the same result.

Selection of Board Members

There are a number of different ways to select board members for a local EDO. Most of them fall into one of the following broad categories:

- Selection by ballot
- Appointment by position in the community
- Selection by membership category
- Selection by executive privilege

Some local EDOs use a combination of these methods. Some use all of them. Which method or combination of methods is used should be clearly spelled out in the EDO's by-laws. Only experience will tell which method or methods work best in a given community. Each method is explained in the paragraphs which follow.

Selection by Ballot

EDOs that use this method elect their board members or, at least, a specified number of them. The process typically works like this. The board appoints a nominating committee that produces a slate of candidates. It is customary to nominate more candidates than the number of open seats. For example, if the board is scheduled to have 10 openings, the nominating committee might recommend a slate of 15 candidates. In addition, provisions are typically made to accommodate write-in candidates.

Ballots are distributed to all members with instructions to choose 10 of the 15 candidates. Some EDOs distribute ballots by mail, others by email, and others in person at their annual meeting. The marked ballots are tabulated by the nominating committee. The 10 with the most votes, including write-ins, are elected. Of course, provisions must be made to break tie votes. A runoff election is one method. However, some boards break ties themselves to avoid the time and expense of a runoff.

Some EDOs ask the nominating committee to offer a slate of candidates equal to the number of open seats. For example, if the board has five openings, the nominating committee recommends five candidates. With this approach, the only alternative members have besides the names on the slate is the write-in vote. On one hand, this approach gives the board more control over its membership. On the other hand, it can have the appearance of "railroading" the election unless the EDO's officers and board members enjoy a high level of credibility with the membership.

My experience suggests that the more involved the membership can be in electing its board members, the better the process will work in the long run. If the EDO's members feel they have no real voice in selecting board members and officers, they will eventually lose interest in the organization.

Appointment by Office

With this method, certain people are selected by virtue of the position they hold in the community. For example, the board might set aside a number of seats to be filled by people who hold such positions as mayor, county commissioner, college president, utility CEO, or any other position that is deemed critical to the board regardless of the individual who currently holds it.

The number of slots reserved for appointment by office selections can vary widely from community to community. Such factors as the size of the community, organizational structure of the EDO, and size of the board must be considered when deciding how many slots to reserve for appointment by office and what the privileged offices should be. Appointment-by-office slots should be reserved solely on the basis of position, not the person who currently holds the position. Further, such slots should be reserved only if the positions in question are critical to the success of the EDO.

Selection by Membership Level

With this method, individuals and businesses that join the local EDO at a specified membership level are either selected automatically as board members or are placed in a pool from which board members are selected. Some EDOs have several different levels of membership, each with its own membership fee and corresponding benefits. For example an individual annual membership might cost $500, a corporate membership $2,000 and a trustee membership $4,000.

With a graduated fee and membership structure such as this, representatives of organizations that join at the trustee level are either: 1) automatically made board members, or 2) placed in a pool from which board members are selected. On one hand, this is an excellent way to provide an incentive for members to join at the highest level. On the other hand, it is not a good idea to allow all board seats to be "purchased." An appropriate balance can be achieved by limiting the number of seats on the board that may be secured in this way. In addition, such positions should be restricted to the large board. Executive board positions are best filled by open elections.

Selection by Executive Privilege

With this method, several seats on the board are reserved for selection by executive privilege. It is the privilege of the EDO's executive board to fill these seats. The number of seats reserved for selection by executive privilege should be kept small so as to avoid charges of cronyism and favoritism. However, giving the executive board the authority to hand-pick a small number of members can empower it to solve several problems occasionally faced by EDOs.

For example, one problem that surfaces from time to time occurs when a loyal member of the EDO works long and hard hoping to win a spot on the board, but still falls a few votes short. Using its executive privilege, the executive board can rectify this situation and keep a committed member from becoming discouraged. Another problem occurs when a certain community leader who is not on the board is going to be essential to the success of a major project the EDO plans to undertake in the coming year. For example, a member of your EDO might be a colleague or friend of a business that is considering opening a new branch plant in your community. Having this member on the board—if only for one year—might increase the EDO's chances of turning a major prospect into a relocation.

Another problem that comes up from time to time is the dues-paying member who opposes a specific project the board has decided to pursue. In such cases it can be better to bring the disgruntled member into the tent than have him outside spreading dissent. Service on the board will give this individual a closer look at and better understanding of the project in question. This might turn the dissenter into an advocate. However, even if it doesn't, maintaining a dialogue with the dissenter is still better than to isolating him. Isolating a dissenter typically just hardens his opposition and encourages him to recruit other dissenters.

Giving a dissenter a seat at the table is also a good way to identify issues and weaknesses the board has overlooked. After all, his reasons for opposing a given initiative might be legitimate or, at least, worthy of consideration. Sometimes interacting on the board with supporters of an initiative will convince a dissenter to temper his opposition or, at least, confine it to board meetings.

Few local EDOs use just one method for selecting board members. Most use a combination of the methods presented herein. I recommend this approach. A hybrid selection system tends to capitalize on the strengths of the methods chosen while minimizing the weaknesses.

Ex-Officio Board Members

Ex-officio members of the board participate fully with two exceptions: they do not vote nor do they hold office. They are selected for membership by virtue of their positions. For example, the EDO's president and CEO is typically an ex-officio member of the board. Selecting others who might serve in an ex-officio capacity depends on the structure of the board and the exigencies of the community. Having a specified number of ex-officio seats on the board is another way to involve critical community leaders who for some reason have not been selected on another basis or who have served their allowable number of terms on the board.

Removing Board Members

One of the most sensitive actions the board of a local EDO can take is the removal of a board member. Unfortunately, this type of action may be necessary on occasion. Consequently, you and your fellow board members should be prepared for it. An important aspect of the board's responsibility is developing guidelines for removing board members and putting those guidelines in the EDO's by-laws.

The guidelines should specify in clear and concise language the reasons a board member can be removed. This is important because the act of removal cannot be allowed to be the result of a member's popularity, opinions, or opposition to a given initiative. Board members must feel free to speak out, voice dissenting opinions, and oppose certain projects; provided, of course, these things are done within the proper channels of the EDO. Doing these things outside of the EDO's established procedures is another matter. Commonly adopted reasons why board members might be removed include the following:

- *Poor attendance.* Board members must lead and in order to do so they must be present. An EDO's board does not need absentee members whose sole reason for joining is to add another line to their resume or to check off a box on their to-do list for career advancement. Consequently, it is wise for the EDO to establish attendance requirements and place them in the by-laws. Failing to meet these requirements is then considered grounds for removal.

- *Conduct that is detrimental to the EDO.* Disagreements among board members are common. This is a fact of life in economic development. As long as those who disagree do not become disagreeable, there is no problem. However, when board members act out their disagreements in ways that are detrimental to the EDO or take any other action that undermines the integrity or mission of the EDO, the board must take action. If informal actions fail to stop the detrimental behavior, the board must take formal action. Typically, boards require a two-thirds majority vote to remove a board members. Some EDOs require a three-fourths majority. Requiring more than a simple majority protects members from arbitrary or capricious action while still giving the board the ability to remove a member for egregious conduct that is detrimental to the EDO.

- *Failure to pay dues.* Private funding for EDOs typically comes in the form of membership dues. Consequently, it is important that board members set the right example by paying their dues on time. Board members who fail to pay their dues promptly will have no credibility when asking other members to pay theirs. Those who do not pay within the specified period should be removed from the board.

BUDGET AND FINANCE

Although it takes more than money to have an effective EDO, money is an important factor. Sufficient funding will not guarantee success in economic development, but insufficient funding can guarantee failure. In order to hire a competent economic development professional as the organization's CEO, the local EDO must be able to offer a competitive salary and benefits package. In order to have an effective marketing program, the local EDO must have the necessary funds in its budget. In order to undertake recruitment and retention programs, the EDO must be able to cover its costs. All of these things as well as the EDO's everyday operating expenses require money.

How much money does it take to have an effective EDO? The answer to this question depends on several variables including the following:

- Size of the community served
- Vision of the EDO's board
- Priorities of the EDO

- Comprehensiveness of the EDO's programs
- How and where the EDO is housed (facility)
- Size and structure of the EDO (staff)

There are no hard and fast rules concerning how much money a community must invest in order to have an effective EDO. However, I recommend the following rule of thumb: *an EDO will need at least $3.00 or more per capita of community population.* In other words, if a local EDO serves a community of 200,000 people, it will need a budget of at least $600,000 annually, and more is better. Of course, this assumes a comprehensive EDO with retention, expansion, start-up, and marketing programs. Also, this rule of thumb is to help you, as a board member, arrive at a ballpark figure. There are successful EDOs that manage to operate without this level of funding and there are those that have more but still do poorly. The $3.00 per capita figure as a minimum is a good starting point for determining the amount of financial support a local EDO will need to do the job expected of it.

The budget should be established annually, monitored carefully, and reported on regularly. A budget update should be a standing item on the agenda of all board meetings. A member of the EDO's paid staff should be responsible for day-to-day bookkeeping duties. This person should, in turn, work closely with the volunteer leader elected to serve as the EDO's treasurer. It is important to have a board member serve as the EDO's treasurer because in the final analysis the board is responsible for the fiscal integrity of the EDO.

COMMITTEES

Local EDOs use committees composed of volunteer members to do much of the work of the organization. Many of the on-going responsibilities of the EDO's board are assigned to committees. These responsibilities include membership development, member retention, business retention, budget development and monitoring, business recruiting, marketing, maintaining an up-to-date inventory of available sites and buildings, supporting new business start-ups, and nominating individuals to serve on the board. Some of the board's committee's are permanent or *standing committees* while others are temporary or *ad hoc committees*. Not only do committees help the EDO perform its work, they get a broad cross section of the EDO's members involved in that work, and getting your members involved is one of the keys to successful member retention.

Standing Committees

Standing committees are permanent, but their members are not—they rotate periodically. The actual number or percentage of members rotated each year and at what intervals should be explained in the EDO's by-laws. Standing committees are like the EDO's board in that they should benefit from an appropriate balance between new and experienced members. The types of standing committees typically established in local EDOs include the: 1) board's executive committee (or executive board) which consists of the EDO's officers and a specified number of board members; 2) membership development committee which is responsible for recruiting and retention of the EDO's members; 3) budget committee which works with the board's treasurer and the staff bookkeeper to formulate and monitor the EDO's budget; 4) business recruiting committee which works with the EDO's staff to plan for prospect visits and to carry out those visits; 5) marketing committee which works with the EDO's staff to develop and implement a comprehensive marketing plan; and 6) sites and buildings committee which works with the EDO's staff to maintain an up-to-date inventory of all available sites and buildings in the community. These are just examples of commonly established committees. A local EDO should base its committee structure on what is best in terms of carrying out its overall economic development program.

PROGRAMS

An EDO's overall economic development program consists of several specific programs. These specific programs go by a variety of different names in different EDOs, but regardless of what they are called in your organization, most will fall into one of the following categories:

- Business attraction (recruiting)

- Business retention and expansion

- Business start-up

- Marketing

- Research

- Inquiry response (from suspects and prospects)

ACCREDITATION PROCESS FOR LOCAL EDOS

Once an EDO is established, properly organized, adequately staffed, and sufficiently funded, the next major challenge is to continually improve—to get better all the time at the process of economic development. One way to formalize and structure the continual improvement process is to pursue accreditation through the International Economic Development Council's "Accredited Economic Development Organization" program. The benefits of formal accreditation include: 1) recognition as an organization of excellence in economic development, 2) critical third-party evaluation of your local EDO, and 3) on-going monitoring of the EDO's status to ensure against a decline in quality.

The IEDC's accreditation process proceeds in two steps: 1) an intensive review of a specified list of documents, and 2) an on-site peer review. Before explaining these two steps, a caveat is in order. Pursuing formal accreditation is one way to help your local EDO continually improve, and it is an excellent way. However, it is not the only way. Some local EDO's choose to establish their own-results oriented benchmarks and use them as the basis for measuring improvement over time. Which of these approaches is ultimately selected must be a local decision, but the boards of local EDOs are well-advised to adopt a system—local or third-party—for ensuring continual improvement. What follows is the information you need to know, as a volunteer leader, about what happens in the formal accreditation process.

Document Review

Local EDOs interested in pursuing accreditation are required to provide a list of documents to the International Economic Development Council (IEDC) for review. These documents typically include the following:

- Articles of incorporation (if applicable)
- By-laws (make sure they are up-to-date)
- Strategic plan
- Annual report (most recent)
- Minutes of meetings for at least the last year
- List of all officers
- Position descriptions for all officers
- Organizational chart for the paid staff
- Policy and procedures manual
- Job descriptions for all positions in the organizational chart
- Marketing plan
- Recent marketing and advertising materials
- Annual budget
- Audited financial statements (most recent)
- Newsletters (most recent editions)
- Press releases (most recent)
- IRS letter of exemption and other applicable IRS forms
- CEO's contract or other evidence of a formal commitment

These documents and any others the IEDC's staff might request are reviewed carefully. If they are found to be acceptable, a team is formed or an individual is selected to make an on-site visit to the EDO. If there are problems with the EDO's documentation, an IEDC representative will work with the EDO to resolve them. The on-site visit is not scheduled until the paperwork review is successfully completed.

On-Site Review

The on-site review typically requires two days. The person or persons conducting the review are all economic development professionals. In other words, IEDC accreditation is the result of a peer review process; one of is best benefits. On-site reviewers are volunteers—they are not paid. The on-site review is designed to be a non-threatening, collegial process in which peers conduct a thorough and objective evaluation.

The on-site review is built around seven broad categories of criteria. Those categories are: 1) internal environment—the office environment in which the staff works everyday; 2) chief executive officer—credentials and experience of the CEO; 3) management and support staff—experience, credentials, and commitment of the support staff; 4) leadership—quality of the volunteer leaders of the EDO; 5) direction and vision—strategic plan for the EDO; 6) external environment—the EDO's relationships with the community, local elected officials, and community leaders; and 7) financial resources—the EDO's budget and sources of income.

After the On-Site Review

After the on-site review has been completed, members of the accreditation team meet to compare notes and decide on a recommendation. Before sending their recommendation to the IEDC, the team conducts an out-briefing with the organization's CEO so that there are no surprises. The team's recommendation is just that—a recommendation. The final decision to award or withhold accreditation is made by the IEDC's board of directors. The actual award is made at the IEDC's annual conference or at a mutually agreed on local community event.

Final Thoughts on Accreditation

Should you, as a volunteer leader of your local EDO, encourage the board to pursue formal accreditation? The best answer I can give you concerning this question is an unqualified maybe. First, you should not assume there is anything wrong with your EDO if it is not accredited. Some of the best local EDO's I have worked with have chosen not to pursue accreditation. On the other hand, accreditation is one way to help a good EDO get even better.

In my work with local EDOs over the past 30-plus years, I have found that EDOs choose to pursue or not pursue accreditation for a variety of different reasons. Reviewing some of the following reasons may help you decide whether or not your EDO should pursue formal accreditation:

- Several EDOs I have worked with chose to pursue accreditation as a way to move up to the next level in economic development. These EDOs were experiencing success and thought that going through the accreditation process might challenge them to do even better.

- Several EDOs I have worked with chose to pursue accreditation as the result of poor performance. These organizations were not doing as well as the board thought they should, but no one could put his finger on the reasons why. These EDO's thought the accreditation process—even if they failed to win accreditation initially—would help identify the factors that were holding them back.

You now have some guidelines that can be used to determine if your EDO is structured for success. The information presented in this chapter should not be viewed as exclusively definitive. Rather, as a volunteer leader, you should apply common sense in using it to determine if your EDO's structure allows it to efficiently and effectively pursue its mission.

Chapter Four

▪▪
▪▪

HIRING AN ECONOMIC
DEVELOPMENT PROFESSIONAL

CHAPTER OUTLINE

▪ Establish and orient the selection committee

▪ Establish hiring criteria

▪ Develop the job description

▪ Advertise the position

▪ Review applications

▪ Conduct interviews

▪ Negotiate the employment contract

I know a civic entrepreneur who has served on the boards of local EDOs in several different communities over the past thirty years. This outstanding community leader believes that the only real job of the local EDO's board is to hire and fire the organization's CEO. While I do not agree that these two duties comprise the only job of an EDO's board, I do agree that they are two of the board's most important duties.

Hiring an economic development professional to serve as the CEO of your organization is similar to manufacturing a product in that the better the process, the better the result. This chapter explains a process that works well when the volunteer leaders of the local EDO need to hire a CEO for the organization. The process consists of the following steps:

- Establish and orient the selection committee
- Establish hiring criteria
- Develop the job description
- Advertise the position
- Review applications
- Conduct interviews
- Negotiate the employment contract

ESTABLISHING AND ORIENTING THE SELECTION COMMITTEE

The selection committee is a critical component in the overall hiring process. A good selection committee is one comprised of members who share one common goal: hiring the best economic development professional the EDO can attract and afford. The selection committee should be chaired by a member of the EDO's board. This is an important appointment because the individual named to chair the selection committee has primary responsibility for all aspects of the process from that point forward.

The ultimate success of the process rests, in large measure, on the shoulders of the committee chair. Because of this, it is not uncommon for the EDO's board chair to also serve as chair of the selection committee. The steps for establishing the selection committee are: 1) prepare to select committee members, 2) select and appoint committee members, and 3) conduct the orientation meeting.

Preparing to Select Committee Members

Getting the right people to serve on the selection committee is critical because the committee will either select a CEO on behalf of the entire organization or, at least, make a recommendation to the board concerning who that person should be. Consequently, the selection committee should be comprised of members who: 1) have the best interests of the EDO at heart, and 2) will devote the time and effort necessary to effectively complete the selection process.

Before selecting committee members, the chair should review the EDO's by-laws paying special attention to those sections covering the selection process. It will be important to ensure that all actions of the selection committee comply with the EDO's by-laws. If you are the chair of the selection committee or a member of it, keep in mind that today's society is litigation-prone. Then act accordingly. You do not want the committee's actions, decisions, or recommendations to be challenged on the basis of procedural errors.

Once the committee chair is well-informed concerning all by-laws governing the selection process, the next step is to develop a list of potential committee members.

A good starting point is the EDO's membership roster. However, it is a good idea to identify members of the board and the EDO at large who, by virtue of their position in their career field, are accustomed to interacting with executive level personnel. Volunteers who are CEOs or executives in their own organizations typically make good selection committee members because they know what it takes to succeed at the executive level and they have the experience to recognize the necessary traits in people who apply to be the EDO's chief executive.

Appointing Committee Members

Committee members should be formally appointed in a letter from the EDO's board chair. However, before writing the letter it is a good idea for the board chair to contact each potential member of the selection committee to make sure he or she is willing to serve. The board chair should make sure that potential members of the committee understand the commitment required and what will be expected of them. All who are willing to make the commitment to serve receive a letter from the board chair. Anyone who is uncertain about making the required commitment should be scratched from the list of potential committee members and replaced with someone else. The selection committee is a working group—something potential members should understand. It should have no honorary members.

Conducting the Orientation Meeting

The appointment letter sent to members of the selection committee should explain in general terms the responsibilities of the committee. The purpose of the orientation meeting is to take the next step: conducting a thorough and detailed discussion of everything the committee members need to know in order to be effective participants in the selection process. Remember, applicants for the CEO's position will probably have a list of very specific questions to ask the committee before and during their interviews. It is important that members of the selection committee be able to give informed, intelligent answers to these questions. Consequently, information presented to selection committee members during the orientation meeting should include the following:

- *EDO's Strategic Plan.* All members of the selection committee should be able to articulate the organization's vision and mission as well as its long and short term goals. It is also a good idea to ensure that committee members are familiar with the strengths, weaknesses, opportunities, and threats at the heart of the strategic plan.

- *EDO's History.* An astute applicant will be interested in the EDO's history. When was the organization established and by whom? How has the EDO developed over time? What are some of the more important historical milestones for the organization? How long did the last CEO stay and why did he leave? What is the relationship of the EDO with other development oriented organizations (i.e. chambers of commerce, downtown redevelopment boards, etc.)? Members of the selection committee should be able to answer these types of questions.

- *Budget.* Astute candidates will want to know the financial condition of the EDO, its sources of funding, if there is a reserve fund and, if so, its current balance, and any budget related problems he or she might face. Most candidates will ask for a copy of the budget as part of the application process and will have studied it and formulated their questions well before the interview. Consequently, members of the selection committee should be prepared to explain the numbers on the page, and any relevant background information.

- *Organizational chart.* Candidates will want to know how the EDO is structured. They may also ask members of the selection committee for their perceptions concerning staff members who currently fill positions in the organization. Whether or not to answer this type of question is something the committee should decide before conducting interviews. My advice to selection committees is to let the new CEO form his or her own opinion of incumbent personnel by avoiding this type of question. Providing job descriptions for the various positions in the organizational chart and explaining which positions are currently filled is acceptable.

- *Policy manual.* Astute candidates will ask for a copy of the EDO's policy manual before arriving for an interview. Consequently, all members of the selection committee should review the policy manual prior to conducting interviews.

- *Membership.* Candidates will be keenly interested in the EDO's membership. How many members are there currently? Is the membership growing, stagnating, or declining? What is the dues structure for members? Are there any membership-related issues or problems at the moment?

- *Programs and initiatives.* Candidates will want to know about the EDO's on-going programs such as marketing, existing industry, recruiting, new business start-ups, etc. They may also want to know about any initiatives the EDO has underway with prospects, expansion of existing companies, or new business start-ups. It will be especially important for members of the selection committee to be able to speak in detail about any initiatives that are currently underway since the new CEO will have to take responsibility for leading these initiatives.

- *Compensation.* Candidates will be keenly interested in compensation-related questions. Consequently, members of the selection committee should be able to speak in detail about such issues as salary, incentives, retirement plan options, health insurance, life insurance, deferred compensation, car allowance, and any other aspects of the EDO's compensation package. In today's high-cost environment, health insurance is a major consideration for candidates. Some EDO's enhance their ability to provide competitive insurance options for the CEO by taking advantage of group programs available through state-level economic development organizations. Other perquisites that are sometimes used to make the compensation package more attractive are payment of professional dues, tuition reimbursement for college courses, time off for professional development, and paid club memberships.

- *Personnel issues.* Candidates will want to know how much authority they have regarding personnel. Are there any "scared cows" on the staff? Does the CEO have final authority with regard to hiring and firing of personnel? This is an important issue because the proper relationship in an EDO is this: 1) the board hires and fires the CEO, and 2) the CEO hires and fires the staff. If this relationship does not exist or if there are any scared cows on the staff, the better candidates may find this unacceptable. On the other hand, an EDO is not a college football team in which the new coach automatically fires all existing coaches and brings in his own staff. My advise to selection committees is that they encourage a new CEO to wait at least six months before making any personnel changes. The authority to make changes should rest with the CEO. However, members of the EDO's staff—especially long-serving members—sometimes have loyal supporters on the board or in the community. Summarily dismissing such individuals can disrupt the smooth operation of the organization. Consequently, it is a good idea for the selection committee to encourage the new CEO to wait an appropriate amount of time before making major personnel decisions.

A Final Word on Orienting the Selection Committee

From the previous section it should be obvious that the members of the selection committee have to review and absorb a lot of detailed information—much more than a volunteer leader typically has to know. One way to lessen the burden for members of the selection committee is for the chair to divide up the responsibilities. With this approach, the chair assigns one member of the committee the responsibility for reviewing the strategic plan, another for the EDO's history, another for compensation, and so on. Then, during interviews, the individual assigned responsibility for any specific aspect of the EDO—strategic plan, budget, compensation—answers questions from candidates in that area.

I recommend a modified version of this approach. With my approach, all members of the selection committee review the material provided in all of the pertinent areas, but not in detail. Then, the chair assigns each specific element to a member of the selection committee. This member will answer detailed questions that fall in his or her area, but all members of the selection committee will have at least a basic working knowledge in all areas.

ESTABLISHING SELECTION CRITERIA

When using a committee to hire a CEO, it is a good idea to make sure that all members understand what the organization is looking for; that everyone is applying the same criteria when reviewing applications. These criteria—once established—should be used by all individuals who review applications and who participate in interviews. Widely-used criteria for hiring economic development professionals include the following:

- In-depth knowledge of all pertinent aspects of economic development (i.e. recruiting, retention, start-ups, and expansion).
- Basic knowledge of the community (out-of-town applicants must do the research necessary to gain this knowledge prior to an interview).
- Proven record of marketing success.
- Business, industry, or other economic development-related experience.
- Good management skills.
- Good communication and human relations skills.
- Ability to interact well with local elected officials.

In some cases there will be other criteria the EDO's board may wish to add to this list. Often there are local issues that dictate the need for specific skills on the part of the CEO. When this is the case, these additional skills should be added to the list. A widely-used approach for developing the list of selection criteria is to have the selection committee develop a draft list and submit it to the EDO's board. The board may approve the list as submitted or revise it. In either case, the final list should be the one approved by the EDO's board.

DEVELOPING THE JOB DESCRIPTION

Once the hiring criteria are established and approved, they can be used to develop a job description. The job description should contain all of the hiring criteria, but it should also contain such additional information as educational requirements, authority of the CEO, responsibilities of the CEO, relationship of the CEO to the board, relationship of the CEO to the staff, and salary range. As with the hiring criteria, the selection committee should develop a draft job description and submit it to the EDO's board for approval.

ADVERTISING THE POSITION

Some EDOs use the "shotgun" approach when advertising for a CEO. They advertise in newspapers, with employment agencies, and in the media. I recommend against this approach. Economic development is a highly specialized profession. Consequently, the "rifle-shot" approach typically works better than the shotgun approach. By rifle-shot approach, I mean advertising in those sources that are connected directly with professional economic developers.

One excellent source is the International Economic Development Council (IEDC). This is the national professional organization for economic development professionals. The IEDC's website address is: www. iedconline.org. The IEDC can help the selection committee plug directly into a network of economic development professionals.

There are also state-level professional organizations for economic development that can be easily located by conducting a quick Internet search. Advertising through these organizations will not only put the EDO in direct contact with economic development professionals, it will multiply the impact of your advertising because economic development professionals who read it will contact others they know who might be in the market for a new or better job.

REVIEWING APPLICATIONS

Selection criteria were established earlier and used in developing a job description. The selection committee should now use this list of hiring to rank all applications received. In the event that an unmanageable number of applications is received, the selection committee chair might wish to appoint two or three members to sort through them to weed out the more marginal candidates. The applications deemed worthy of the committee's attention are then rated using the selection criteria as the basis. The top candidates make up the committee's "short-list" of applicants to be offered an interview.

CONDUCTING INTERVIEWS

Before inviting candidates to interview, the committee must decide whether or not it will pay travel expenses for applicants who accept the invitation. This can be an expensive undertaking for an EDO and, as a result, deserves careful thought. On one hand, requiring applicants to pay their own travel expenses might limit the number of qualified candidates interviewed. On the other hand, paying travel expenses might encourage less serious applicants to accept an interview when, in fact, they are not likely to take the job if offered. What follows are several strategies that can be used to deal with this dilemma:

- Conduct telephone interviews before inviting candidates in for a face-to-face interview. This step can help validate the committee's interest in a candidate or point out problems that did not show up during the application review process.

- Check references carefully before inviting a candidate to a face-to-face interview. This step can help validate the committee's interest in a candidate or point out problems that did not show up during the application review process.

- Offer to reimburse candidates who come for a face-to-face interview half of the travel expenses. The candidate who is eventually selected is reimbursed for the other half when he or she accepts and begins work. Candidates who are willing to pay half of their own travel expenses are likely to be serious about the position. I recommend reimbursing the successful candidate for the remainder of travel expenses only after an agreed upon period of time has elapsed because I have seen situations in which a new CEO accepted a job and kept it for only a short period of time before moving on to another position. In a case like this, the EDO has exhausted its budget for selecting a new CEO but must still go through much of the process again. At the very least, it is wise to build a hold-back clause into the new CEO's contract to cover this contingency.

This last scenario in which a candidate accepts the CEO position but quickly leaves is not that uncommon. For this reason, and because the highest rated candidate might not accept the position when it is offered, I recommend that the selection committee rank at least its top three candidates after the interviews have been completed. In this way, the number two candidate can be offered the job without the expense of conducting additional interviews should the number one candidate turn the position down or accept it and then quickly leave.

Another important issue for interviews is the questions that are asked of candidates. To ensure objectivity during interviews and to prevent potential legal and procedural challenges to the EDO's eventual hiring decision, I recommend the selection committee develop a list of questions to be asked of all candidates interviewed. In this way, all candidates are asked the same questions. This does not mean that members of the selection committee cannot ask follow-up questions or additional questions for clarification. Rather, it means that all candidates get the opportunity to answer the same basic questions, thereby giving the members of the selection committee a better basis for making comparisons.

NEGOTIATING THE EMPLOYMENT CONTRACT

I recommend providing a formal employment contract for CEOs. For one reason, the better candidates for the position will expect one. For another, a contract is more professional. It will help prevent the kinds of problems and misunderstandings associated with verbal agreements. Before interviewing any candidates, the selection committee should have gained board approval on the following issues: 1) compensation range for negotiating the actual salary, 2) details for paying any remaining reimbursement costs associated with the interview, 3) cash bonuses and incentives, 4) insurance (life, medical, disability, etc.), 5) retirement plan, 6) deferred compensation if applicable, 7) automobile or automobile allowance, and 8) various perquisites.

Hiring a CEO in economic development is an inexact science at best. However, the procedures recommended in this chapter can help produce optimum results. Some of what is explained in this chapter might differ somewhat from the procedures used to hire key decision makers in your organization. If this is the case, do not hesitate to recommend strategies you have found effective. Your experience is part of what makes you a valuable asset to the EDO. Explain your recommendations, gain buy-in from the selection committee, win approval from the board, and implement your strategies.

Chapter Five

███
███

STRATEGIC PLANNING FOR ECONOMIC DEVELOPMENT

CHAPTER OUTLINE

- Rationale for strategic planning
- Overview of the strategic planning process
- The pre-planning process
- The EDO's vision for the community
- The mission statement
- The guiding principles
- The S.W.O.T. analysis
- The strategic goals
- The execution plan

Strategic planning can help a local EDO in two ways. First, the strategic planning process results in a product that can serve as the organization's roadmap for success. Second, just going through the process can be an invaluable growth experience for the EDO's volunteer leaders. Strategic planning is about envisioning a desirable future—in this case for the community served by the local EDO—and laying out a roadmap that will guide the community to that future.

RATIONALE FOR STRATEGIC PLANNING

If done well, the strategic planning process can serve a number of purposes for a community and its local EDO. The more important of these purposes are explained in this section.

Creates a Clear Vision for the Future

Adults like to ask young people the following question: "What do you want to be when you grow up?" Often young people have trouble answering this question because they are so involved in the day-to-day aspects of their lives that they simply have not thought about it. The same thing happens in communities. Community leaders can become so wrapped up in their day-to-day work and personal lives that they forget to ask what they would like their community to be when it "grows up."

Strategic planning is a process that allows communities and the EDO's that serve them to answer this fundamental question: "What kind of community do we want to have in the future." Until this question is asked and answered, local communities are like a person walking along a path with his eyes on the ground paying little attention to where he is going. Remember, on any journey, before you can figure out how to get there you must first decide where you are going. Strategic planning helps communities decide where they are going.

Provides a Mechanism for Developing Community-Wide Consensus

Economic development cannot take place in a vacuum. The more support there is from the community, the better the concept works. Strategic planning gives local EDOs a mechanism for bringing a broad cross-section of stakeholders to the table, giving them opportunities to participate in charting their community's future, and gaining consensus concerning what that future should be. By going through the process with a broad cross-section of stakeholders, the EDO can gain community-wide consensus on a vision for the future while, at the same time, identifying potential roadblocks to achieving that vision.

Provides a Reality Check for Community Leaders

A good strategic plan is not a "pie-in-the-sky" document containing a compilation of unrealistic dreams. Rather, it should be what I call a *realistic stretch document*. On one hand, it should be realistic in that the goals it contains are attainable. On the other hand, it should require the community to stretch in order to achieve those goals. Balance between the real and the ideal is critical in strategic planning. Set your sights too low, and the resulting plan will fail to spark excitement in stakeholders. Set your sights too high, and stakeholders will feel over-whelmed. In either case, they will lose interest. The strategic planning process gives a community the opportunity to set its sights on a better future that is both highly desirable and practically attainable.

OVERVIEW OF THE STRATEGIC PLANNING PROCESS

The first thing you need to know about strategic planning for economic development is that it differs in one major way from strategic planning for businesses and other types of organizations. The strategic plan for a local EDO is not just for the organization itself, but for the community served by the EDO. In a practical sense, this means that the vision developed as part of the process is a vision for the community, not for the EDO. The EDO's mission, then, becomes to help achieve this community vision for economic development.

The strategic planning process should proceed in a systematic, step-by-step manner. Since each step in the process depends on the one that precedes it, the various steps should be undertaken in order. These steps are as follows:

1. Complete the pre-planning process

2. Create the vision

3. Develop the mission statement

4. Develop the guiding principles

5. Conduct the S.W.O.T. Analysis

6. Develop the strategic goals

7. Execute the strategic plan

THE PRE-PLANNING PROCESS

Before beginning the strategic planning process, there are several tasks that must be completed. Completing these tasks will help ensure an effective strategic planning process. Pre-planning tasks are as follows:

- Select the members of the strategic planning team and decide who will facilitate

- Develop a schedule and budget for the process

- Arrange to involve a broad base of stakeholders in the process

Forming the Strategic Planning Team and Naming a Facilitator

The best strategic planning team for a local EDO is broadly representative of the organization's board and membership. This means that the team should have members from the EDO's board, its various committees, and the membership at large. There are no hard and fast rules concerning the appropriate number of members for the strategic planning team, but I have experienced the best results with teams of eight to ten people. More than ten can become unwieldy, while fewer than eight can result in under-representation.

Remember, input into the plan is not confined to members of the strategic planning team. The team does most of the work of drafting the plan. However, as is explained in the next section, other stakeholders are given opportunities to comment on the draft and make recommendations for additions, deletions, and revisions. These other stakeholders include members of the EDO's membership as well as the community at large.

An important part of forming the strategic planning committee is naming a facilitator. The facilitator is not actually a member of the team. Rather, this individual is responsible for assisting the team's chair in getting the planning process organized, recording the team's work, and keeping all aspects of the planning process flowing smoothly. The facilitator becomes especially important during meetings in which other stakeholders are given opportunities to provide input. The facilitator has no direct input into the process. Rather, this individual acts as the master of ceremonies, keeping the process flowing smoothly, discussion on track, and debate constructive. When disagreements among participants become disagreeable, the facilitator is responsible for calling a timeout and gently prodding participants to rein in their emotions.

Develop a Schedule and Budget for the Process

Once the strategic planning process begins, it will be important to keep it on schedule or people will lose interest. Developing the schedule for the process is the job of the strategic planning committee. When developing a schedule, remember to factor in the following events and activities:

- Developing the first draft of the plan.
- Electronically circulating the draft plan among all members of the EDO and compiling their feedback.
- Revising the draft plan based on feedback from the EDO's membership.
- Presenting the draft plan to a broad base of stakeholders through town hall meetings.
- Revising the draft plan as necessary based on stakeholder input.
- Presenting the final plan to the EDO's board for approval.
- Conducting the implementation ceremony.

The amount of time allotted for each of these activities must, of necessity, be determined locally. However, I recommend completing the entire strategic planning process in no more than three months.

Once the schedule has been finalized, the committee must develop a budget to cover any expenses associated with developing the strategic plan. The schedule is a good guide for determining what costs will be associated with the plan. Typically, the EDO's staff will be tasked with supporting the various phases of the plan's development (e.g. typing and re-typing drafts, emailing drafts to members, handling the logistical aspects of town hall meetings, making copies, etc.). If this is the case, the EDO might simply absorb these costs as part of its normal operation. However, if outside administrative support is needed, it must be planned for in the budget. On occasion it might be necessary to rent facilities for town hall meetings. In addition, it is a good idea to provide water, soda, tea, and coffee for participants during these meetings.

How much time is allotted each of these activities as well as the preparation time that must precede each activity must, of necessity, be a local decision. However, I recommend completing the entire process from start to finish in three months or less. Dragging the process out too long just invites opposition and controversy. Cutting the process off too soon limits feedback.

Determine how to Involve a Broad Base of Stakeholders

An EDO's strategic plan is developed for the community served. Consequently, it is important to give members of the community input into the process. It is also important to give members of the EDO's membership and board who are not selected to serve on the strategic planning committee opportunities for input. Because involving a broad base of stakeholders in the process will typically slow the process and almost always complicate it, some EDOs are tempted to limit involvement to those selected to serve on the planning committee.

Having served as a strategic planning consultant for numerous EDOs, I can certainly understand the desire to keep the process simple by involving the minimum number of stakeholders. After all, the concept of too many cooks in the kitchen is a valid concern. The more people involved, the more likely it is that the process will get bogged down by naysayers, nitpickers, and participants who just like to hear the sound of their own voices. However, a strategic plan for economic development cannot be kept secret. The final plan will eventually surface, and when it does the naysayers who were left out of the process will probably be even more vocal than they would have been if involved from the outset. This is why I recommend a practical approach that involves a broad base of stakeholders, but minimizes the frustrations associated with doing so.

With this approach, the strategic planning committee develops a draft plan. The draft is then circulated electronically among all members of the EDO. Members are given a stated period of time to submit comments, questions, concerns, and recommendations. Once the feedback from members has been compiled and dealt with—included in the plan, rejected, or returned for clarification—the revised plan is circulated among the EDO's members one more time. After any additional revisions that may be necessary are made, the plan is ready for public comment.

This is potentially the most frustrating phase in the planning process. The strategic planning committee and its facilitator should work together to schedule town hall meetings. The general public is invited to attend these meetings and offer input. The number of meetings depends on the size and make up of the EDO's service region. For example, if the EDO serves a multi-county region, there may have to be multiple meetings at locations that are convenient to all constituents. The rule of thumb to follow when deciding how many town hall meetings to have and where to have them is this: *make at least one meeting convenient to every geographic area in the EDO's service region.*

Town hall meetings are attended by all members of the strategic planning committee and emceed by the committee's facilitator. All major components of the draft plan are presented to those in attendance. The facilitator records input on flip charts and refers questions to members of the committee. The facilitator's job is to keep the meeting moving while, at the same time, making sure participants get a chance to provide input. This means the facilitator must encourage all to participate, but allow no one to dominate.

The approach I have found most effective in facilitating town hall

meetings for EDOs is to present each component of the plan to participants and, then, listen. I encourage strategic planning committee members to suppress the temptation to rationalize, justify, or defend the plan
when it is challenged by people in the audience. Rather, they should all
answer the questions asked as succinctly as possible, but avoid getting
into debates or disagreements with participants. It is better to just let
participants have their say and get anything that is bothering them off
their chest. It has been my experience that challenging town hall participants just intensifies their opposition and encourages others to jump on
the bandwagon. Rather, the facilitator and committee members should
simply listen, record all input provided, thank participants, and ensure
them that their recommendations and concerns will be given serious
consideration.

In most town hall meetings I have facilitated for local EDOs, there
will be input from the audience that is rational, logical, and worthy of
further consideration. However, it has also been my experience that
many of the people who attend town hall meetings are similar to those
who make a hobby of attending county commission and city council
meetings—they have an axe to grind, an agenda to advance, or something they want to say. Such participants want to be heard, and nothing
will satisfy them but to be heard. With this type of participant, discretion is the best course. It is not likely that reason, logic, or common
sense will change their thinking or convince them to consider another
point of view. Consequently, allowing them to vent is the best course.
Often, having the opportunity to voice their opinions publicly is more
important to these types of participants than the eventual outcome of
the issue.

THE EDO'S VISION FOR THE COMMUNITY

Most strategic planners and strategic planning guides recommend conducting the SWOT analysis before developing the vision. I used to
recommend this approach myself. However, after working with local
EDOs for many years as a strategic planning consultant, I came to real-

ize that developing the vision should be the first task undertaken after the pre-planning phase of the process. This is because the vision provides the context for all other phases of the strategic planning process. For example, when the committee conducts the SWOT analysis, the various strengths, weaknesses, opportunities, and threats identified should be viewed from the perspective of the community's vision. A certain factor is a strength only if it can help move the community toward realization of its vision. Correspondingly, an apparent shortcoming is a weakness only if it inhibits progress toward realization of the vision. Opportunities and threats should also be identified within the context of the vision.

A community's dream for its economy and quality of life should be apparent in the EDO's vision statement. A vision should be a metaphoric beacon in the distance toward which the community is always moving. Everything about the strategic plan and the corresponding structure of the EDO should support the ultimate realization of the vision. In a community with a clear vision, it is much less difficult for the EDO to stay focused. If an activity does not move the EDO closer to attainment of the vision, why have it? If a policy does not support attainment of the vision, why adopt it? If an expenditure of resources does not help achieve the vision, why make it? If a position or department in the EDO does not support the vision, why have it?

Writing the Vision Statement

A well-written vision statement, regardless of the size and nature of the community should answer such questions as these. What would we like our community to become? What would we like our community to be when it "grows up"? A vision statement should answer these types of questions and have the following characteristics:

1.   Easily understood by all stakeholders

2.   Brief yet clear and comprehensive in meaning

3.   Challenging yet attainable

4. Lofty yet tangible

5. Worthy of the time and effort of stakeholders

6. Capable of creating unity of purpose among stakeholders

7. Not concerned with numbers, percentages, or other quantitative data

The following vision statements are examples from EDOs I have worked with over the years. The community names have been changed, but the statements have not. Each of these examples satisfies the seven criteria listed above.

- Smithville will be a thriving community with a balanced economy, high-value jobs, and an attractive quality of life.

- Jones County will have a stable economic base with an appropriate balance between tourism and manufacturing and the highest quality of life in the region.

- Millville will be the premier community in the panhandle—a community of cooperative people working together to continually improve the economy, develop the necessary infrastructure, protect the environment, and maintain a high quality of life.

- Gracetown will be a community of diverse, cooperative people willing to pool their resources to ensure positive economic growth, excellence in education, and environmental integrity while maintaining a small town atmosphere and quality of life.

- Bakersfield will be the best small town in the state in which to live, work, and do business. Our highest priorities are the local business climate and our quality of life.

- Walford County will have the most vibrant, balanced, and rapidly growing economy in the southeast while maintaining its historic small-town values and quality of life.

All of these sample vision statements are easily understood by stakeholders because they are brief, to the point, and clear in meaning. At the same time each vision statement is comprehensive enough to cover a wide range of economic development activities. In fact, the only limitations placed on the EDOs of these communities are that while developing the economy, they are to protect the environment and quality of life in the communities they serve.

All of these sample visions are challenging, but attainable if the respective communities are willing to put forth a consistent and concerted effort. All of them are lofty in that they aim high, but not so high that they are intangible. These are tangible, understandable, attainable visions. All of the visions are capable of stirring excitement among stakeholders. After all, who wouldn't want a thriving economy, clean environment, and high quality of life? Finally, all of these visions set a positive, "can-do" tone for their communities without using numbers or percentages.

WRITING THE MISSION STATEMENT

The mission statement for a local EDO should describe why the organization is in business. It should answer such questions as: 1) What is the EDO's purpose? 2) Why does the EDO exist? and 3) What is the EDO's service area? In answering these questions, the mission statement should satisfy the following characteristics. It should:

- Describe what the EDO does and where (service area)
- Be brief, but comprehensive (one paragraph should be sufficient)
- Be easy to understand, but descriptive
- Avoid *how-to* statements

The following mission statements are those of various EDOs I have worked with over the years. The names of the communities have been changed, but the mission statements have not. Each mission statement satisfies the criteria listed above.

- The mission of the Murdock County Economic Development Council is to focus the community's energy, expertise, and resources on continually improving the local economy while simultaneously maintaining a desirable quality of life. Major activities of the EDC include: retention, expansion, and recruitment of businesses; facilitation of the start-up of new business startups; and enhancement of education, recreation, and culture.

- The mission of the Jayville Economic Development Council is to channel community resources in such as way as to build a progressive, diversified, environmentally positive economic base. Major activities include maintaining and expanding existing businesses, attracting new businesses, and promoting the start-up of locally grown businesses.

- The mission of the Oakview Economic Development Council is to create an ever growing number of high-value jobs, continually improve the local business climate, and promote on-going enhancements to the community's quality of life.

Each of these mission statements describes what the EDO in question does and where. The *where* component of the mission in each case is part of the EDO's name (e.g. Murdock County EDC, Jayville EDC, and Oakview EDC). The *what* component is explained in brief, but comprehensive terms that can encompass a wide range of economic development activities and initiatives. Each mission statement is written in terms that are easy to understand without resorting to the use of *how* statements.

DEVELOPING THE GUIDING PRINCIPLES

Guiding principles establish the framework within which the EDO will pursue its mission. In the private sector, guiding principles are more commonly known as *corporate values.* Each guiding principle represents an important core value of the EDO. Together, all of the guiding principles represent the EDO's corporate value system. Guiding principles come into play on a practical level when the EDO's board must make difficult decisions. All decisions of the board and staff should be informed by the organization's guiding principles and made in accordance with those principles. What follows are sample guiding principles taken from the strategic plans of various EDOs I have worked with over the years:

- *Integrity.* We will adhere to the highest ethical standards and encourage honesty and trust.

- *Harmony.* We will maintain an appropriate level of harmony between economic growth and such concerns as environmental protection, quality of life, and infrastructure loading.

- *Economic diversity.* We will maintain an economic base that is appropriately diverse so that we avoid becoming overly dependent on any one sector.

- *Environmental sensitivity.* As we undertake economic development initiatives, we will be sensitive to protecting the community's natural resources and environment.

- *High-value jobs.* Our focus will be on creating not just jobs, but high-value jobs.

- *Sector focus.* We will focus our efforts on attracting, expanding, and creating businesses in the manufacturing, engineering, and aerospace sectors.

- *Community involvement.* We will keep the community involved in and informed about all economic development initiatives.

These few guiding principles are provided as examples. The actual principles adopted as well as the number of principles will vary from community to community. The list of guiding principles is complete when it represents the core values of your EDO and its community concerning economic development.

THE S.W.O.T. ANALYSIS

Some consultants conduct the S.W.O.T. analysis as the first step in the strategic planning process. However, I hold off on this step until the EDO has a vision, mission, and guiding principles. My reasoning is simple. The community's strengths, weaknesses, opportunities, and threats should be identified, viewed, and recorded from the perspective of the organization's mission, vision, and guiding principles. A good lead-in to help set the right tone for the S.W.O.T. analysis is this: *If this is our mission and our vision and these are our guiding principles, what are our strengths, weaknesses, opportunities, and threats in relation to them.* In other words, the mission, vision, and guiding principles provide the context for deciding whether a given factor is in fact a strength, weakness, opportunity, or threat.

I encourage EDOs to conduct the S.W.O.T. analysis within a specific framework by figuratively looking in a mirror and asking specific questions within several broad categories of concern. These categories are as follows: 1) community commitment, 2) local government support, 3) physical infrastructure, 4) leadership capacity, 5) organizational structure, 6) labor force, 7) collaboration, and 8) miscellaneous. Suggested questions in each of these categories are provided in the following paragraphs. These questions are provided to help trigger the thinking of members of your EDO's strategic planning committee. However, they should not be considered comprehensive. Questions may be added or eliminated depending on the exigencies of local communities and EDOs.

Community Commitment

The questions in this section of the S.W.O.T. analysis are asked to determine the extent to which the overall community is committed to and supportive of economic development.

1.   Is there community-wide buy-in to the EDO's vision for economic development?

2.   Is there a positive attitude in the community about economic development?

3.   Do existing businesses fear that economic development will create labor shortages or wage inflation?

4. Are there organized citizen's groups that oppose economic development?

5. Do local citizens frequently express concerns about traffic congestion, overcrowding, urban sprawl, an overloaded infrastructure, etc. at county commission or city council meetings?

Local Government Support

Because local government agencies typically control a community's infrastructure, EDOs must have the support of local elected officials in order to successfully pursue economic development initiatives. The questions in this section of the S.W.O.T. analysis help determine the extent to which government support for economic development exists.

1. Do local government bodies have a positive, supportive attitude toward economic development?

2. Are local government bodies willing to provide an appropriate level of funding to support economic development?

3. Are local government bodies willing to provide competitive financial incentives such as tax relief to support specific economic development initiatives?

4. Do local elected officials play an active role in economic development (e.g. serve on the board of the EDO, help host prospect visits, etc.)?

5. Do local elected officials help create a positive attitude among their constituents in the community toward economic development?

Physical Infrastructure

One of the most commonly made errors in economic development is allowing development projects to overload the infrastructure. This happens when economic development proceeds faster than infrastructure development; a problem that often occurs because the private sector can usually move faster than the public sector. In spite of the differing paces of progress associated with the two sectors, physical infrastructure is an important element in the economic development of a community. The questions in this section of the S.W.O.T. analysis will help you determine whether the community's physical infrastructure is an economic development asset or a liability.

1. Are roads and bridges in the community in good condition and do they have the capacity to support growth?

2. Are curbing, gutters, and drainage in the community in good condition and do they have the capacity to support growth?

3. Are sewer systems in the community in good condition and do they have the capacity to support growth?

4. Is the potable water system in the community in good condition and does it have the capacity to support growth?

5. Is the natural gas system in good condition and does it have the capacity to support growth?

6. Is the electrical distribution system in good condition and does it have the capacity to support growth?

7. Is the telecommunication system in good condition and does it have the capacity to support growth?

8. Does the community have a fully developed business, commerce, or industrial park available and does it have the capacity to support growth?

9. Does the community have sufficient undeveloped land available to accommodate commercial and residential growth?

10. Does the community have one or more "spec" buildings available for immediate occupancy by a new or expanding business?

11. Is there vacant commercial space available in the community and does the EDO have an up-to-date inventory of the space?

Leadership Capacity

The quality of local leadership in both the private and public sectors is an important issue in economic development. The questions in this section of the S.W.O.T. analysis will help determine if local leadership is an asset or a liability.

- Are local elected officials willing to help fund economic development?

- Are local elected officials willing to provide competitive incentives to help attract, retain, and develop business?

- Are local elected officials willing to keep permitting, zoning, and other regulatory requirements reasonable?

- Are local elected officials willing to help expedite approval of regulatory permits when necessary?

- Are local elected officials willing to help the EDO build and maintain a broad base of community support for economic development?

- Are key community leaders and opinion makers willing to contribute financially to support economic development by paying dues and participating in other resource development activities?

- Are key community leaders willing to devote their time and expertise to economic development?

- Are private and public sector leaders willing to work together cooperatively in support of economic development?

- Are public and private sector leaders willing to put aside their personal agendas for the greater good of the overall community?

Organizational Structure

An important part of a community's ability to undertake responsible economic development is having an efficiently and effectively functioning EDO. The questions in this section of the S.W.O.T. analysis will help determine if the EDO, as currently structured and operating, is an economic development asset or a liability.

1. Does the community have a functioning EDO?

2. Does the EDO have a competent economic development professional as its CEO?

3. Does the EDO have adequate office space to house its staff and carry out its duties?

4. Does the EDO have up-to-date technologies sufficient to support its mission?

5. Does the EDO have a sufficient number of competent support staffers?

6. Does the EDO have an active, committed, effective board of directors?

7. Does the EDO have an adequate, dependable budget that is sufficient to carry out its mission?

8. Does the EDO have positive working relationships with all stakeholders in the community?

9. Does the EDO have a comprehensive strategic plan for economic development?

10. Does the EDO have effective, on-going programs for business retention, expansion, recruiting, start-ups, and marketing?

Labor Force

The availability and quality of the labor force is always a major consideration for prospects who might consider your community. The questions in this section of the S.W.O.T. analysis will help determine whether the local labor force is an economic development asset or liability.

1. Is there a sufficient supply of trained or, at least, trainable people in the community to provide an immediate labor force for new businesses without requiring that they draw employees from existing firms?

2. Are there effective education and training programs available lo-

cally to create a pool of potential employees that is continually maintained at an acceptable level?

3. Are there effective continuing education and training programs available locally for updating and retraining people?

4. Are opportunities available locally for customized training programs provided on site for businesses?

Collaboration

A willingness to collaborate on the part of stakeholder organizations in the community is an important concern in economic development. The questions in this section of the S.W.O.T. analysis will help determine if stakeholder organizations in the community are willing to collaborate on economic development initiatives.

1. Are other not-for-profit organizations that have a stake in economic development willing to collaborate with the EDO on economic development initiatives?

2. Are local government agencies willing to collaborate with the EDO on economic development initiatives?

3. Are critical private sector organization such as utility companies willing to collaborate with the EDO on economic development initiatives?

4. Are local education agencies and organizations (K-12 and higher education) willing to collaborate with the EDO on economic development initiatives?

Miscellaneous

There are a number of concerns relating to economic development that do not fall comfortably into any of the broad categories just presented. Questions in this section of the S.W.O.T. analysis cover those concerns and are no less important because they are grouped together as "miscellaneous" issues. In fact, some the questions asked in this section deal with issues that are essential to successful economic development at the local level.

1. Does the community have any natural resources that could be considered economic development assets?

2. Does the community's location offer the advantage of market proximity for businesses in a given sector?

3. Does the community have local sources of business capital sufficient to support growth?

4. Does the community offer proximity to dependable transportation systems (major highways, railroads, airports, seaports, etc.)?

5. Are there climate-related issues that might impede economic development (annual closing days for snow, tornadoes, hurricanes, etc.)?

6. Does the community offer quality education systems at the K-12 and college levels?

7. Are personal, property, and business tax rates reasonable and competitive?

8. Are property insurance rates reasonable and competitive?

9. Are there trends or changes occurring locally, regionally, or nationally that could present opportunities or threats to the economic well-being of the community?

Answering these questions in a straight-forward and honest manner will help the strategic planning committee identify the community's strengths, weaknesses, opportunities, and threats relating to economic development. This information is then used to develop broad strategic goals. However, before proceeding to that step, a word of caution is in order.

A Final Word of Caution About the S.W.O.T. Analysis

In working with local EDOs over the years, I have found that convincing people to be open, honest, and constructively critical—especially when trying to identify weaknesses and threats—is the most difficult part of the S.W.O.T. analysis. Civic entrepreneurs and community leaders who serve on the boards of local EDOs tend to be positive people—they typically see the glass as being half full. As a result, they like to put their best foot forward when describing their community by emphasizing the positive and down playing the negative.

Consequently, it is important for the facilitator and other members of the strategic planning committee to be aware of this positive propensity and take appropriate action when they see it. When I facilitate strategic planning sessions for organizations, I begin the S.W.O.T. analysis with the following message: "The S.W.O.T. analysis is not a marketing exercise. Rather, it is an introspective, self-critical enterprise in which identifying weaknesses and threats is as important as identifying strengths and opportunities." This point needs to be stressed throughout the analysis process by members of the strategic planning committee as well as the facilitator.

It is far better to identify a weakness during the S.W.O.T. analysis and take steps to mitigate or correct it than to cover it up and have a prospect discover it during a visit to the community. As hard as it can be to bring the community's shortcomings out in the open, it is essential to do so. A community does not have to be perfect in order to succeed at economic development—no community is—but it does have to be honest with itself and prospects. During the development of broad strategic goals, planning for the correction of weaknesses and mitigation of threats is an important part of the process; just as important as exploiting strengths and opportunities.

STRATEGIC GOALS

The beginning point for developing strategic goals is the S.W.O.T. analysis. The strategic planning committee is not limited to using only the results of this analysis for developing strategic goals, but these results should be the starting point. Strategic goals should be written to take advantage of the community's strengths, correct weaknesses, exploit opportunities, and mitigate threats.

When working with EDOs on strategic planning, I often find that participants do not understand what a strategic goal is. Members of the strategic planning committee often want to immediately set such goals as these: 1) attract two new companies per year, 2) expand one existing firm per year, and 3) facilitate the start up of two companies per year. These are *result* goals not *strategic* goals. Strategic goals set the stage for the accomplishment of result goals—they create the conditions and capacity that are necessary for the accomplishment of result goals. This is why it is important to use the S.W.O.T. analysis as the beginning point for developing strategic goals.

For example, assume that one of the weaknesses identified in the S.W.O.T. analysis was a negative attitude in the community toward economic development. The planning committee would want to develop a strategic goal for turning this negative situation around. Such a goal might read as follows:

> *Create and maintain a positive attitude toward economic development among a broad base of local stakeholders.*

This is a strategic goal because it is aimed at creating the conditions in which economic development can be successfully undertaken. Specific actions to be taken to achieve this strategic goal are not part of the strategic plan. Rather, specific actions are identified and recorded during the development of the EDO's annual plan of work (explained in the next section of this chapter). The annual plan of work is also where result goals are recorded.

Strategic goals are broadly stated—so broadly that they might never be completely achieved. In other words, they are the type of goals toward which progress should be made every year, but with additional progress still possible in successive years. Take the earlier example of *creating and maintaining a positive attitude toward economic development among local stakeholders.* No matter how much progress is made in a given year in creating a positive attitude among stakeholders, the number of stakeholders who support economic development can probably be still be increased the next year and the next and the next. Also, even if it were possible to gain the unconditional support of every stakeholder in a community, that support would still have to be maintained.

With this characteristic of strategic goals in mind, review the examples that follow. These are strategic goals taken from the plans of local EDOs I have worked with over the years. All of these goals were excerpted from an EDO's S.W.O.T. analysis.

- Gain the support of local citizen groups that currently oppose economic development to gain their support.

- Win the support of the county commission for providing on-going funding for economic development.

- Persuade local elected officials to expand the community's waste water treatment capacity sufficiently to support growth.

- Persuade the gas company to expand its distribution system to include the new technology and commerce park.

- Convince the local military base to cede ownership of a 300 acre tract of land to be used as the site for a technology park.

- Win the support of the county commission for the establishment of competitive economic development incentives aimed at new and expanding companies.

- Convince the community's "top-tier" business leaders to become active members of the EDO.

- Identify a competent, experienced economic development professional who can take the EDO to the next level as its CEO.

- Work with Johnson Community College to establish a corporate training center for providing customized training for the personnel of local companies.

- Convince all local chambers of commerce to partner with the EDO for the betterment of the community.

Adopting result goals relating to the strategic goals and identifying the specific actions that will have to be taken in order to achieve them happens in the next step—developing the execution plan.

THE EXECUTION PLAN

What I call the *execution plan* is not actually part of the strategic plan. However, after helping private, public, and not-for-profit organizations develop strategic plans for more than 30 years, I have learned a valuable lesson. Unless you take the next step and develop an execution plan, the strategic plan is likely to just sit on a shelf and gather dust. This is because a strategic plan is, by definition, broadly stated. Consequently, its implementation is everybody's responsibility.

The problem with the strategic plan being everybody's responsibility is that until specific aspects of a plan are assigned to specific individuals with specific deadlines, nothing gets done. Everybody just waits for someone else to do something. Because not-for-profit organizations such as local EDOs typically get a new board chair and at least some new board members every year, there is always the danger of the organization simply reliving the same year over and over again year after year. To avoid this organizational tendency, I recommend using the board's annual plan of work as an implementation plan. The annual plan of work consists of the goals and actions to be completed in a given year. These goals and actions should be tied directly to one or more of the EDO's broad strategic goals.

With this approach, the EDO moves ever closer to the realizations of its vision each year as the current board picks up where the last board left off. This concept of each successive board standing on the shoulders of its predecessors is how EDOs continue to grow, develop, and make progress over time. The planning steps are as follows.

1.   Each year the new board examines the EDO's strategic plan and decides which of the strategic goals it would like to focus on in the coming year.

2. The board then discusses specific actions that can be taken during the coming year to move the EDO closer to the accomplishment of the strategic goals selected. The key to success is to strike an appropriate balance between being realistic and stretching.

3. Specific actions that are to be taken relating to the strategic goals are recorded. Then individuals (typically committee chairs) are assigned responsibility for these specific actions.

4. Meetings are arranged with those who are assigned responsibility for given actions so that a realistic timetable can be developed. The results of these meetings are tentative deadlines the responsible parties and their committees will work to meet.

5. All of the actions to be taken during the upcoming year, the individuals assigned responsibility for them, and deadlines for completion become the board's plan of work for the year in question.

The annual plan of work then serves as an implementation plan for the EDO's strategic plan. The following example of how a strategic goal serves as the basis for more specific action as part of an annual plan of work illustrates the critical relationship between the strategic and implementation plans.

Strategic goal:

Increase the level of support in the community for economic development.

Specific actions, responsible parties, and deadlines:

1. Develop a comprehensive DVD presentation entitled "The Benefits of Economic Development." This action is assigned to Mack Jones, Chair of the Marketing and Public Relations Committee. The video is to be ready for use no later than April 10th.

2. Schedule a series of "townhall" meetings in which the DVD "The Benefits of Economic Development," will be shown and a panel consisting of the CEO and five selected board members will answer questions. This action is assigned to Jane Meadows, Board Chair. The meetings are to be scheduled and the panel selected no later than April 15th.

3. Handle the logistical details of setting up and advertising the townhall meetings. This action is assigned to Andrew Torre, Operations Vice-President of the EDO. Logistical arrangements are to be completed no later than April 15th.

The information in this chapter will help you and other volunteer leaders play a positive role in developing a comprehensive strategic plan for your EDO. It will also help you take the additional steps necessary to ensure that the strategic plan is effectively implemented.

Chapter Six

BUSINESS ATTRACTION

No aspect of economic development gets more attention than business attraction. In fact, business attraction is what most people think of when economic development is the topic of discussion. Having read earlier chapters in this book, you know that business attraction is just one of the building blocks in a comprehensive economic development program. Never the less, even if sometimes given more attention than it deserves, business attraction is an important aspect of any economic development program.

OVERVIEW AND PURPOSE OF BUSINESS ATTRACTION

Business attraction is often referred to as "recruiting" because so much of the process is wrapped up in just that. However, in reality, recruiting represents just the marketing and hosting elements of business attraction. There is much more to business attraction than just recruiting. As a volunteer leader of your EDO, you need to understand the overall process, its purpose, and the role you play in it.

The overall process involves: 1) understanding what your community has to offer prospects (this was determined by the S.W.O.T. analysis during the strategic planning process), 2) targeting businesses in selected sectors that might find the community's assets attractive (e.g. manufacturing, defense contracting, engineering, sports teams, corporate headquarters, research and development, large-scale retail, etc.), 3) marketing the community directly to the targeted sectors, 4) establishing positive working relations with site selection consultants that specialize in the targeted sectors, 5) maintaining comprehensive prospect files for on-going follow-up and relationship building, 6) hosting on-site prospect visits, and 7) facilitating the relocation of prospects that choose your community. Volunteer leaders can play important roles in all of these various elements of the process.

Regardless of the business sectors targeted by your community, business attraction, is an economic development strategy that can and should serve the following purposes: 1) create new high-value jobs, 2) enhance the community's tax base, 3) diversify and, in turn, help stabilize the community's economy, 3) enhance the quality of life in the community, and 4) mitigate the "brain drain" problem (occurs primarily in small communities where the best and brightest must leave in order to find rewarding employment).

MAJOR OBSTACLE TO SUCCESS IN BUSINESS ATTRACTION

There is one overriding obstacle to success in economic development: competition. Economic development is one of those games that everyone plays, and plays to win. Every community, city, and county in the U.S. is looking to enhance its economy, quality of life, and tax base. This fact, alone, makes for intense competition. However, in this age of globalization, competition is not limited to communities in the U.S. Certain types of businesses are now just as likely to locate in India, China, Mexico, or other emerging nations as they are in the U.S. Hence, competition in economic development has become global.

Add to this the increasing use of creative incentives, and you will find that economic development is one of the most competitive enterprises in the world. It is not uncommon for a community in say Northwest Florida to find that it is competing against other communities not just in Alabama, Mississippi, and Georgia, but also in South America, Central America, China, Indonesia, Malaysia, Korea, India, South Africa, and one or more of the former Soviet republics. The message here is to think broadly and prepare your community to compete globally.

ROLE OF SITE SELECTION CONSULTANTS

Choosing to relocate to or open a new branch in a community is a major decision for a company. Consequently, most prospects approach the site selection process with great caution, as they should. One of the ways companies try to reduce their risk when considering a relocation decision is to contract with a site selection consultant. Site selection consultants are experts at building bridges between companies that have specific, well-defined needs and communities that can meet those needs. A site selection consultant is the economic development equivalent of a match maker.

Because they are so often the first point of contact between a prospect and a community, site selection consultants should be identified and targeted as part of the EDO's marketing program. By identifying site selection consultants that specialize in targeted business sectors, and establishing positive working relationships with them, communities can improve their chances of being introduced to prospects on a regular basis. Site selection consultants are easily identified through the International Economic Development Council (IEDC) and its state-level affiliates.

FACTORS PROSPECTS CONSIDER WHEN MAKING LOCATION DECISIONS

The most effective members of the teams EDOs put together to host vis-iting prospects are those volunteers who can think like a prospect, volun-teers who know what a prospect is looking for. By targeting certain types of businesses—adopting a sector strategy—rather than simply trying to attract any type of business, EDOs make it easier to think like a prospect. This is because the needs of sector specific businesses are well-defined and similar regardless of the location in question.

For example, a manufacturing firm will need: ample water, gas, elec-tricity, and sewer capacity; a readily available supply of affordable em-ployees who are skilled or, at least, trainable; manufacturing facilities that are available or can be built at competitive per square foot costs; reason-able taxes and manufacturing-related regulations; and access to specified types of transportation (truck, rail, air, and/or water). A corporate head-quarters, on the other hand, will be more interested in quality of life, cultural amenities, educational opportunities for the families of managers and employees, access to dependable air transportation, and state-of-the-art telecommunications capabilities. Regardless of business sector, the needs of prospects can be grouped into several categories.

Geographic Needs

Some businesses need to be located in geographic proximity to either their customer base or the suppliers of their raw materials. Others need to be located in proximity to specific transportation routes such as inter-state highways, international airports, railroad depots, or sea ports. These are all considered geographic needs.

Site Needs

Some businesses need a level site. Others, such as microchip manufac-turers, need sites that are not just level, but have solid, stable soil condi-tions free from ground vibrations that might undermine the integrity of the manufacturing process. Room for ample parking is almost always a site-related concern. Some businesses prefer a secluded site while others need a site that can be easily viewed from nearby highways.

Facilities

Facility related concerns include such things as immediacy of availability (this is why some communities build "spec" buildings), cost per square foot, type (manufacturing, office, retail, etc.), quality, location, and access to utilities.

Workforce

Workforce related concerns almost always include such factors as: 1) size of the available labor force, 2) quality of the labor force (skilled, semi-skilled, unskilled), 3) union or non-union orientation, 4) cost (wage expectations), and 5) prevailing work ethic.

Capital and Incentives

Access to capital is usually an important consideration for prospects. The availability and cost of venture capital, investors, and bridge loans are all important factors. Incentives such as tax abatement, no-interest loans, and cost waivers are also important considerations for many prospects.

Education

Education related considerations are two-fold. Prospects will be interested in having access to the resources and amenities of colleges and universities and specialized research laboratories. They will also be interested in the quality of education available for their children and the children of employees at all levels; K-12 through college.

Natural Climate

Prospects will want to know if the climate is conducive to year-round work or if the community is prone to work interruptions that result from hurricanes, tornadoes, snowfall, ice storms, or any other climate-related conditions. The community's average number of work days per year is typically an important statistic.

Business Climate

The state of the business climate is always a concern to prospects. Is the business climate positive or negative, pro-business, or anti-business? Are business taxes high or reasonable? Are zoning regulations overly-restrictive or reasonable? Do local government agencies inhibit or assist businesses?

Quality of Life

With some businesses, quality of life is the most important concern— even if that fact goes unstated. Recreational activities, cultural amenities, the crime rate, the availability and quality of social services, the quality and cost of housing, fire protection, law enforcement services, and the overall cost of living are typically important factors for prospects. Never underestimate the effect the quality of life in your community can have on economic development. I was once involved with a prospect that had done everything but sign the final relocation paperwork, when, at the last minute, the CEO of the company in question backed out because his wife balked at moving to a community that had no ballet, opera, and or symphony.

COMMUNITY AND SITE PROFILES

Community and site profiles are among the most important tools available to local EDOs. Consequently, time, energy, and money spent developing and maintaining comprehensive profiles for the community and for specific sites within the community are resources wisely. Community and site profiles answer the types of questions prospects and site selection consultants have when they begin their search for a new location. There was once a time when answering these types of questions was the responsibility of the prospect's site selection team. However, competition among community's trying to attract new businesses now demands that EDOs get out in front and answer a standard set of questions for prospects.

EDOs that fail to develop comprehensive community profiles and make them available electronically on an up-to-date web site are not likely to attract many prospects. Community profiles provide information about the community in general. Site profiles contain information relating specifically to a building or site that is immediately available for either occupancy or development.

Community profiles should be developed to answer questions that prospects are likely to ask in all of the following key areas of concern: facilities, workforce, capital/incentives, education, natural climate, business climate, and quality of life. The needs of prospects in these key areas were explained in the previous section. In addition to generic community information, profiles of specific sites are important. Site specific profiles should contain at least the following information for each individual site that is available in the community for immediate occupancy or development:

- Physical aspects of the site (e.g. location, size, slope, drainage, zoning status, expansion capacity, current use, empty/occupied, compatibility with nearby facilities and neighborhoods, stability of the soil, etc.).

- Ownership (e.g. current owner of the site, status of the title, easements, etc.).

- Site preparation status (e.g. clearing and grading requirements, remediation required, etc.).

- Cost of the site (e.g. asking price, hidden costs, terms, etc.).

- Utilities (e.g. types available, immediacy of availability, cost, installation costs, etc.).

- Transportation (e.g. access to highway, railroad, air, and sea transportation as well as the cost of improving access, etc.).

- Public services (e.g. law enforcement, fire, fire insurance rating, emergency operations, etc.).

■   Natural climate (e.g. average annual rainfall or snowfall, torna-
dos, hurricanes, floods, etc.).

The categories of information recommended in this section should be
viewed as the minimum to be provided. This information and any other
information that is pertinent to the community in general or to any specific site within the community should be kept up to date continually.
It should also be presented in an attractive, professional, easy-to-access
manner on the EDO's web site.

COMMUNITY MARKETING

Marketing is a broad concept that consists of putting the community in a
position to succeed. It involves creating a positive image for the community, identifying the various assets of the community, and using a variety
of strategies for reaching out to businesses in targeted sectors that might
like the image and need the assets. Marketing, as it relates to economic
development, uses the community as its product and the assets of that
community as its message.

Marketing in economic development is more effective when undertaken in a focused, direct manner. The "shotgun" approach is typically
not effective. Also, glitz and glitter do poorly as marketing strategies
in economic development. Marketing materials—brochures, DVDs,
web sites—should be professional in appearance, but when marketing a
community the content of the book is more important than the cover.
Site selection consultants and members of site selection teams will be
more impressed with marketing materials that provide solid, dependable answers to pertinent questions than with glamorous, but shallow
materials that attempt to cover up weaknesses with attractive words and
high-quality graphics.

The EDO's web site is probably its most important marketing tool.
Site selection consultants and members of site selection teams will typically go to the EDO's web site before deciding whether or not to contact
anyone in person or by telephone. If they don't like what they see on the

web site, it is unlikely they will even take the next step. Consequently, it is critical to have an attractive, professional design for the EDO's web site, keep the information on the web site up to date, and make sure the information presented is comprehensive.

Accessibility and convenience are important. Never force prospects to work hard to find what they need on your web site. Use the web site yourself. I talk to economic development volunteers all the time who have never visited their EDO's web site. Pretend you are a prospect looking for a new location. Is the information you need conveniently accessible? Is the information you need available and up to date? What information is not on the web site that would be helpful to you? If there are problems or areas that could be improved, let the staff know.

The EDO's web site should contain all of the information from the community profile and individual site profiles explained earlier in this chapter. In addition, the following information will be welcomed by prospects:

- Links to education agencies and organizations; training providers; sources of capital; providers of cultural, recreational, and leisure activities; local government agencies; other community-based organizations; and workforce development boards.

- Biographies of selected EDO staff personnel, board members, and committee chairs.

- Applications for permits, loans, zoning changes or exemptions, and other pertinent processes.

- A community calendar of events and activities.

- Local publications.

- Air travel information.

- Shopping information.

An innovative web-based tool for marketing specific sites is a Geographic Information System (GIS). A GIS system can record all factors relating to a given geographic area and present it in pictorial form accompanied by all relevant statistics. A GIS system can show everything that is on, under, and above the ground for a given site as well as such pertinent information as climate, demographic, tax, zoning, topographical, consumer, and workforce data relating to the site. It can also show a comprehensive inventory of buildings on the site and every aspect of the buildings (e.g. overall size, cost per square foot, utilities, room sizes, relative condition, ingress and egress, contents, and anything else that might be contained in a set of architectural and engineering drawings and specifications).

ECONOMIC DEVELOPMENT INCENTIVES

Incentives are financial strategies that can lower the cost of doing business for a prospect or existing business. They typically include such strategies as tax abatement and tax credits as well as a variety of in-kind services. With tax abatement and tax credits, prospects that locate in the community receive a reduced tax burden for a specified period of time. With in-kind services, costs are reduced when the community agrees to shoulder the financial burden for any service the prospect would otherwise have to pay for (e.g. infrastructure improvements, workforce screening and training, technical assistance, construction costs, reduced utility charges, permitting assistance/expediting, etc.).

EDO's often have a love-hate relationship with economic development incentives. On one hand, EDOs sometimes love them because they can make the community more competitive. On the other hand, they sometimes hate them because: 1) they are almost always controversial, and 2) it is typically necessary to increase them over time in order to stay competitive.

Economic development incentives can be controversial because: 1) those who oppose economic development like to portray them as "corporate welfare," and 2) EDOs sometimes make the mistake of providing them only for business attraction, thereby overlooking existing business expansion. Those who think of incentives as corporate welfare can be difficult to convince otherwise. In fact, after dealing with this issue for more than 30 years, I am convinced that most people who portray incentives as corporate welfare are really just opposed to economic development in any form and simply use the corporate welfare argument as a way to justify their opposition. In other words, take away the incentives and most of the naysayers would still find a reason to oppose economic development.

The point to be made to those who think of incentives as corporate welfare is that the need for them is rooted firmly in the concept of competition. If other equally attractive communities offer them and yours doesn't, prospects are smart enough to make the obvious choice. However, if your community can offer comparable, carefully planned incentives that pay out only on the basis of performance, it can be competitive in today's global economic development marketplace. Incentives are not about welfare, they are about competitiveness.

Failing to provide comparable incentives to existing businesses that expand is a major source of controversy. Such a practice leaves the EDO open to criticism that it collects membership dues from existing businesses and uses them to recruit new businesses. If this is true, it is a sure way to lose good members. Whatever incentives are made available to prospects should also be made available to existing businesses that expand locally.

PROSPECT VISITS

When a prospect chooses to visit your community, the EDO's staff will pull together an ad hoc committee to host the visit. Membership on this "host committee" is determined by the nature and needs of the prospect. The EDO's board chair typically leads the group with support provided by the organization's CEO. The remaining members are typically volunteers who can speak with authority about concerns or areas of interest the prospect has expressed prior to the visit. For example, if a prospect has a strong interest in K-12 education, the local school superintendent would be asked to join the committee. If financing is an issue, a banker or representative of a venture capital firm would be included. The expressed interests of the prospect should dictate the composition of the host committee.

If you are chosen to serve on a host committee for a prospect visit, there are several rules of thumb to keep in mind:

- Ask the EDO's staff why you were selected (i.e. What role are you expected to play on the committee?).

- Do your research (i.e. Learn as much as you can about the prospect, the specific individuals who will visit the community, your EDO's community and site profiles, and the types of information the prospect might request from you).

- Dress as if you are going to an important job interview.

- Remember your table manners at all meals (I have seen a community lose a prospect as a result of the poor table manners and excessive drinking of a prominent volunteer leader).

- Remember that even the social aspects of a prospect's visit are business. Show prospects your best behavior at all times. The real social activities do not take place until the ink is dry on a relocation contract.

- Be as helpful as you can, but do not appear overly eager. Prospects might misinterpret your eagerness for desperation. Also, if you do not know how to answer a prospect's question, make note of it and get the information later. Do not provide an inaccurate answer or try to wing it with prospects.

Volunteers can play critical roles in the business attraction process. This is one of the areas in economic development in which your professional background can be especially valuable to the EDO. Prospects will want you to take off your EDO hat and put on your professional hat so they can talk business leader to business leader. The information presented in this chapter will help you ensure that the role you play is positive and helpful.

Chapter Seven

▟▛

BUSINESS RETENTION AND EXPANSION

Every business is constantly looking for ways to do two things: 1) increase the amount of business they do, and 2) reduce the cost of doing business. This is why EDOs have business attraction programs. They are trying to find businesses that want to do more business or reduce the cost of doing business by relocating to a different community. The existing businesses in your community are no different. As a volunteer leader of a local EDO, understand that there are EDOs in other communities working hard to attract businesses away from your community. The most important message in this chapter is this: never take your local businesses for granted—they could relocate. Rather, work hard to retain the existing businesses in your community and help them expand.

OVERVIEW OF BUSINESS RETENTION AND EXPANSION

Business retention and expansion is a phrase that encompasses anything and everything a local EDO does to ensure that local business stay in the community (retention) and grow over time (expansion). For example, using the EDO's web site to help local businesses market to a broader audience is a retention and expansion strategy. Intervening with the county commission to ensure that economic development incentives apply as fully to existing businesses that expand as they do to new businesses is a retention and expansion strategy. Working with a local community college to arrange training for an existing business so that it can pursue a new product line is a retention and expansion strategy.

In all but the most exceptional cases, business retention and expansion should be the number one priority of local EDOs. There are several reasons for this: 1) in most communities, existing businesses account for the majority of the jobs that are available; 2) losing businesses to another community can make it even more difficult to attract new businesses; 3) existing businesses pay the membership dues that help fund the local EDO; and 4) it costs less in time, money, and energy to expand a local business than to attract a new one.

PURPOSE OF BUSINESS RETENTION AND EXPANSION

The business retention and expansion efforts of local EDOs serve one broad purpose and several specific purposes; all of which are beneficial to a community. The broad purpose of business retention and expansion is to maintain an environment that is conducive to the long-term success of local businesses; an environment that makes staying in the community good business while simultaneously encouraging expansion. Specific purposes of business retention and expansion include:

- Retaining and expanding the local employment base
- Maintaining a stable local tax base
- Maintaining a stable local economy

- Continually improving the local business environment
- Contributing to the success of the business attraction program

ROLE OF VOLUNTEER LEADERS

Nobody is better able to keep the EDO up to date concerning the needs, circumstances, and current status of existing businesses than the organization's volunteers—many of whom represent existing businesses themselves. Your organization is susceptible to the same types of ever changing socio-economic demands that affect other existing businesses in the community. Chances are good that if your organization is facing a new challenge, so are other existing businesses in the community. Every organization—even during the best of times—needs to find ways to reduce the cost of doing business, improve competitiveness, and increase sales.

The local business environment, infrastructure, labor force, education system, cultural amenities, incentives, and many other factors can affect the cost of doing business, the ability to compete, and the level of sales. This fact is what establishes the most important role of board members and volunteers in business retention: the responsibility to continually look for changes in the local business environment that might have a negative effect on existing businesses. By keeping the EDO's professional staff and board informed concerning the needs of and potential threats to existing businesses, you can play an important role in keeping the organization engaged on behalf of those businesses.

BUSINESS RETENTION AND EXPANSION PROGRAMS

Local EDOs should establish on-going programs that promote retention and expansion on a continual basis. Those that wait until a crisis occurs before getting engaged will have waited too long. Business retention and expansion programs must be a normal part of the EDO's structure and daily operations. These programs should be designed to satisfy one of the following purposes:

- Identifying factors that might cause existing businesses to consider new locations and eliminating or mitigating those factors.

- Providing programs and/or services that will help enhance the ability of existing businesses to compete.

- Providing programs and/or services that will help existing businesses increase sales.

Eliminating Factors That Might Lead to a Relocation

There is no end to the list of obstacles that can increase the cost of doing business for existing firms. Utility costs can increase to uncompetitive levels. The community's infrastructure (i.e. roads, curbing, storm water runoff system, waste water treatment facilities, etc.) can be neglected to the point that demand out paces capacity forcing businesses to make their own improvements. Taxes, impact fees, and insurance costs can increase to a level that is unreasonable. Zoning restrictions can be passed that inhibit growth.

It is the responsibility of the EDO's staff and board to stay out in front on issues that might increase the cost of doing business locally and to take whatever steps are necessary to prevent or mitigate the negative impact of these issues. This means that the EDO must stay in constant touch with all of the organizations and agencies that can affect the local business climate (e.g. city councils, county commissions, state legislature, utility providers, etc.). Staff personnel and volunteer leaders must maintain positive working relationships with key decision makers in all of these organizations and agencies so that the EDO is always in the loop before decisions are made that could have a negative effect on the local business climate.

Being an ever-vigilant advocate for existing businesses is a key role volunteer leaders can play in local EDOs. By coming together under the auspices of the EDO, business and community leaders can join forces and enjoy the benefits of speaking with one collective voice. By doing this, they can multiply the effectiveness of their pro-business advocacy.

Continually Improving the Competitiveness of Existing Businesses

Your local EDO can contribute significantly to helping existing businesses continually improve their competitiveness if the organization's leaders understand the concept of superior value. In a hyper-competitive global marketplace, organizations survive and succeed by consistently providing superior value for customers. Superior value is the result of superior quality, cost, and service.

Anything the EDO can do to help its existing businesses consistently achieve superior value or come closer to doing so will, in turn, improve their ability to compete. But what can an EDO do along these lines? The best thing it can do is build bridges between existing companies and organizations that can help. In this regard, the EDO serves as a facilitator and broker.

By identifying organizations in the region that provide continual improvement-related services and establishing positive working relationships with decision makers in these organizations, EDOs can position themselves to facilitate and broker the types of services existing businesses need to stay competitive. The types of organizations EDOs should partner with include community colleges, technical schools, universities, training companies, workforce boards, and selected consulting firms.

EDOs put themselves in positions to facilitate and broker continual-improvement services by: 1) knowing what types of help existing businesses need, 2) understanding what the various partner organizations can provide, 3) establishing working relationships with key contacts in partner organizations, 4) and bringing together the businesses that need help and the partner organizations that can provide it. The value of brokering and facilitating continual-improvement activities should not be underplayed.

On one hand, existing businesses that struggle to stay afloat in a sea of competition may not have the time to reach out to partnering organizations themselves. On the other hand, partnering organizations stay equally busy with their daily obligations and can always use help with making the right connections in the business community. The following case explaining the relationship between a local EDO and a college is an excellent example of the type of partnership recommended herein.

OWC Corporate Training Center/Okaloosa EDC Partnership

The Okaloosa-Walton College Corporate Training Center (CTC) provides consulting services and training in the areas of leadership, management, supervision, quality, and continual improvement. The CTC's purpose is to help organizations continually improve their people, processes, and products in ways that will continually improve their ability to compete in the global marketplace. This purpose makes the CTC a natural partner with the Okaloosa County EDC since both organizations have an interest in helping existing businesses.

The EDC's role is to market the various services available through the CTC. The college's role is to provide the consulting services and training. Consulting and training are available to any existing business in the community. However, the EDC's members receive a discount on registration fees. Consulting that leads to training is provided at no charge. Training is provided either on site or in college facilities based on the needs and desires of the business in question. Some of the CTC's more frequently requested training programs are:

- Effective leadership (for executives and management personnel)
- Effective supervision (for first-line supervisors)
- Effective teamwork
- Effective change management
- Effective strategic planning
- Effective customer service
- Six Sigma
- Lean Six Sigma
- ISO 9000
- Occupational safety

- Managing the unmotivated
- Opportunity lost: how bad management ruins good employees
- Effective communication in the workplace
- Effective conflict management

The EDC surveys its members regularly to determine what kinds of consulting and training are needed. The CTC continually adds to its roster of competent professionals who can provide the types of training needed. Together the CTC and EDC work as partners to help existing businesses lower the cost of doing business, enhance competitiveness, and increase sales. The information in this chapter will help you, a volunteer leader in a local EDO, play an effective role in the retention and expansion of existing businesses. But, more than anything else, it is your position as a professional in an existing business that will make you effective in this role. Remember, if your organization is struggling with issues that make it difficult to compete or that increase the cost of doing business, other local businesses are probably having the same experience. The most important role you can play in such cases is to alert the EDO so appropriate action can be taken.

Chapter Eight

▪▪
▪▪

TECHNOLOGY TRANSFER

CHAPTER OUTLINE

- ▪ Technology transfer defined
- ▪ Economic development goals of technology transfer
- ▪ Inhibitors of technology transfer
- ▪ Commercialization of technology
- ▪ Diffusion of technology
- ▪ Technology transfer programs

An economic development strategy that is often overlooked by local EDOs is technology transfer. Volunteer leaders in local EDOs should understand technology transfer as a concept as well as how it can be adopted as an economic development strategy.

TECHNOLOGY TRANSFER DEFINED

Technology transfer is the process of moving technology from one setting to another. In actual practice it means: 1) moving a newly developed technology out of a laboratory setting into a commercial setting where it can be produced and marketed, and 2) moving the newly produced technology out of the commercial organization and into the hands of users. The first step in the process—from laboratory to commercial enterprise—is known as the *commercialization* of technology. The second step—from commercial enterprise to users—is known as the *diffusion* of technology. Together, these two steps make up the broader concept of technology transfer.

A technology transfer project I once worked on with a local EDO was based on sound-proofing technology. The sound-proofing material in question had been developed by a military research laboratory for use in lining the helmets of pilots to block out extraneous noise. The material developed was quite thin and very effective. It had a number of obvious commercial applications including noise insulation in automobiles and buildings. The EDO worked as an intermediary in bringing the laboratory and commercial businesses together so that a technology transfer contract could be developed. This is an example of the commercialization step in the technology transfer process.

Wearing my college professor and administrator's hats, I have been involved in the diffusion step of the technology transfer process for more than 30 years. This step is often over looked in discussions of technology transfer, but is a critical step none-the-less. In fact, without it, newly commercialized products would just sit gathering dust on warehouse shelves. A number of factors can inhibit the diffusion of commercialized technologies. One of the most common inhibiting factors is market and user ignorance. In these cases, users either do not know about the technology (market ignorance) or know about it but do not know how to use it (user ignorance). Marketing and training can help bridge the gap that often exists between the commercialization and diffusion steps in technology transfer.

Even when they know about a new technology, potential users may be reluctant to make a purchase if they don't know how to use it. This is one of the reasons off-the-shelf technologies sometimes don't move as fast as their manufacturers would like. For example, I was involved in the early development of computer-aided drafting and design software. The company I served as a consultant had done an excellent job of developing a powerful but affordable software package for drafting and design instructional programs in technical schools and community colleges. However, there was a problem the developers did not anticipate; a serious problem as it turned out. Because the instructors who represented the primary market for the CADD software did not know how to use it, they were reluctant to purchase it. In other words, the technology (CADD software) had been commercialized, but it was bogged down at the diffusion step. This is what led to my involvement.

The developer of the CADD software hired me as a consultant to design a training program for drafting and design instructors that could be presented at professional conferences as well as on-site in their facilities. Once we started helping instructors learn how to use a computer to do what they had always done with a pencil and straight edge, sales soon followed and the business that developed the software eventually did quite well with its new product line.

ECONOMIC DEVELOPMENT GOALS OF TECHNOLOGY TRANSFER

Technology transfer, as an economic development strategy, can be part of the EDO's business retention and expansion and new business start-up programs. An innovative technology transferred out of a research laboratory can be the basis for a new product line for expanding an existing business or starting a new business. Consequently, EDO's that adopt technology transfer as an economic development strategy typically have the following goals:

- Facilitate business start-ups based on the technology.
- Facilitate the expansion of existing businesses on the basis of the technology.
- Facilitate the retention of existing businesses by enhancing their competitiveness through the addition of a new product line or

service based on the technology.

In order to be an effective facilitator of technology transfer, local EDOs must: 1) establish working relationships with research laboratories; 2) arrange on-going opportunities for decision makers in research laboratories and local businesses to interact; and 3) establish working relationships with educational institutions and training organizations that can help with the diffusion step of the process.

INHIBITORS OF TECHNOLOGY TRANSFER

On one hand, technology transfer has great potential as an economic development strategy. On the other hand, the process can be challenging. What follows are several factors that can inhibit the technology transfer process:

- *Vision limitations.* Sometimes the potential commercial applications of a new technology will be obvious. However, this is not always the case. For example, for years the laser was thought of as a solution looking for a problem. It was a powerful, innovative technology, but commercial applications eluded its inventors for years. When Alexander Graham Bell invented what became the telephone, he was trying to develop an aid for teaching the deaf. Scientists in research laboratories are sometimes better at developing new technologies than at finding commercial applications for them. This is why on-going interaction between research personnel and business leaders is so important. With their different but complementary perspectives, scientists and business leaders can help each other get past the visioning limitations inherent in the technology transfer process.

- *Risk aversion.* Technology commercialization is by its nature a risky undertaking. A business that decides to take a chance on commercializing a new technology typically faces a substantial up-front investment that may or may not pay off in the long run. Many business professionals are averse to the level of risk often associated with commercializing a new technology.

- *Too many unknowns.* There are often many unknowns associated with the commercialization of a new technology. Is there a market for the new product? What size is the potential market? Will demand for the new technology be short or long term in nature? Will anyone risk backing the capital investment that will be necessary? Do we have the facility, expertise, equipment, and processes required to manufacture and market the product? Do we know what will be necessary in order to diffuse the new product?

- *Bureaucracy.* Research laboratories tend to be government organizations. As such, their processes and procedures must comply with a myriad of state or federal government regulations or both. Business professionals often find dealing with government bureaucracy frustrating or, at least, confusing. Business professionals will sometimes shy away from the process when they discover all that is involved.

Because of these inhibitors, I always advise EDOs that want to adopt technology transfer as an economic development strategy to name a staffer or appoint a committee of volunteers who are willing to become experts at navigating the process. Anything the EDO can do to save existing businesses and local entrepreneurs time and trouble relating to technology transfer will help facilitate the process. This is the appropriate role of the EDO in the process—facilitator.

COMMERCIALIZATION OF TECHNOLOGY

Commercialization is the step in the technology transfer process that tends to get the most attention. It consists of all the various activities that must be completed to move a new technology out of a research lab, into a commercial enterprise, and make it ready for distribution to users. Typical activities that must be completed as part of the commercialization step of the technology transfer process include the following:

■ Commercialization assessment

■ Establishment of relationships with potential commercial partners

■ Feasibility assessments by potential commercial partners

■ Market research

■ Design and engineering of a prototype

■ Development of a prototype

■ Market testing of the prototype

■ Production of the new product

■ Marketing of the new product

Of these various steps, local EDOs can play a key role in at least the first two. By establishing positive working relationships with research laboratories, local EDOs can gain access to the results of the on-going commercialization assessments that take place in research laboratories. Armed with this type of information, local EDOs can circulate the results of commercial assessments among their existing businesses. When a local business expresses interest in a given technology, the EDO can introduce its representatives to decision makers in research laboratories.

Of course, even if a given business decides to pursue the commercialization of a new technology, there is still much to be done; much that does not typically involve the EDO. However, the EDO's role in the commercialization of technology—though admittedly limited—is still important. If the first two steps in the process are not completed, the commercialization step never gets started. This is why EDOs are well advised to develop the in-house expertise needed to play a positive, facilitating role in the commercialization step.

DIFFUSION OF TECHNOLOGY

The following fictitious case illustrates why technology diffusion can be so difficult. Try to envision a time when cars were a rarity rather than something many families have two or more of. Assume that the automobile was invented in a research laboratory and then transferred from the laboratory to a commercial enterprise. Market research showed that the automobile would be a hugely successful product if it could be mass produced at an affordable price. On the basis of this research, thousands of cars were produced and a creative marketing program was implemented. Unfortunately, in the beginning car sales were not as brisk as the manufacturer needed them to be in order to recover his investment in commercializing the automobile.

Technology commercialization allowed cars to be produced and marketed at a price consumers could afford, but the overall technology transfer process came to a grinding halt at the diffusion step. There were at least two major issues inhibiting the wide-scale diffusion of the automobile: 1) people accustomed to horse and buggy transportation did not know how to drive automobiles, and 2) the supportive infrastructure—paved roads, gas stations, auto repair shops, and automobile dealerships,—did not yet exist. In this fictitious situation, a local EDO could have helped promote diffusion of the automobile by: 1) connecting the automobile's manufacturer with organizations that could provide driver training, and 2) supporting the automobile manufacturer's request to have the county commission start paving roads. These helpful actions would not have solved all of the problems inhibiting diffusion of the automobile, but they would have helped.

There are limits to what a local EDO can do to help with the diffusion step of the technology transfer process, but there are also things EDOs can do to help. Establishing relationships with key personnel in training organizations and bringing them together with representatives of organizations that commercialize technology will help encourage diffusion. This is why forward-looking technology companies such as MicroSoft certify selected educational institutions as official training sites for their products. Representing the interests of businesses with local government agencies when necessary will also help. The key to helping promote effective technology diffusion is for local EDOs to be open to facilitating and brokering when existing businesses run into local barriers.

TECHNOLOGY TRANSFER PROGRAMS

There are a variety of programs that local EDOs can partner with to promote technology transfer in their communities. These include the following:

- *Research Consortiums.* A research consortium is a group of research laboratories and other research-based organizations that come together to promote technology transfer. A typical research consortium might include universities, colleges, private research laboratories, and department of defense/military laboratories. Forming a consortium gives participants opportunities to network, share ideas, discuss problems, and help each other find more effective ways to facilitate the commercialization process. For example, the Gulf Coast Alliance for Technology Transfer (GCATT) is a research consortium in Northwest Florida that includes military research laboratories from Eglin Air Force Base, Pensacola Naval Air Station, Tyndall Air Force Base, Fort Rucker Army Aviation Center (Alabama), the High Magnetic Field Laboratory at Florida State University, the Research-Engineering-Education Facility of the University of Florida, the University of West Florida, and Okaloosa-Walton College. These organizations work together and with EDOs to encourage the commercialization of government sponsored research that leads to new technologies.

- *Centers of Emphasis.* A center of emphasis is a specialized facility that focuses on a specific area of research. For example, the Center for Human and Machine Cognition in Pensacola, Florida specializes in research relating to the interface between people and technology.

- *Seed Capital Organizations.* These are firms that provide funding for start-up firms or existing businesses that hope to commercialize a new technology. Seed capital firms are especially important to the commercialization step of the technology transfer process because traditional lending institutions are often too risk averse to take a chance on a new technology.

■ *Research Parks/Campuses*. A research park—sometimes called a research campus—is an industrial park consisting of research firms rather than industrial or manufacturing firms. Research parks typically bring research-oriented organizations from the public, private, and military sectors together in one location to gain the synergy that can result from their everyday interaction. An example of a research park is the Emerald Coast Research and Technology Campus in Okaloosa County, Florida. The "Campus" consists of such tenants as the University of West Florida, Research-Engineering- Education Facility of the University of Florida, Eglin Air Force Base, Okaloosa-Walton College, and various private research-based firms.

Adopting technology transfer as an economic development strategy requires local EDOs to commit to developing specialized knowledge of the concept and process, either on the staff or through a standing committee. If there are research laboratories in or near the region served by your EDO, technology transfer can be a productive strategy. As a volunteer leader in your EDO, the more you know about the process, the more effective a player you can be in it.

Chapter Nine

██
██

PROMOTING ENTREPRENEURSHIP AND BUSINESS STARTUPS

Entrepreneurs are people who find innovative solutions to unmet needs and, then, take the risk necessary to transform their solutions into businesses. Consequently, entrepreneurs create jobs. In fact, most new businesses in the U.S. are small businesses established by entrepreneurs who take a chance on an idea for meeting an unmet need and reach out to a niche market with what they hope will be a solution. This fact makes entrepreneurs and local EDOs natural allies. Another fact—that most new jobs created in the U.S. are in small businesses of less than 500 employees—just cements the relationship that should exist between entrepreneurs and local EDOs.

LOCAL EDOS AND ENTREPRENEURSHIP

Local EDOs can play an important facilitating role in promoting entrepreneurship in their communities. Perhaps the best way to understand this role is to consider what I call my "clearing-the-road" analogy. In this analogy, the entrepreneur is trying to move a truck load of important goods down a bumpy, pothole-filled road from Point A to Point B. It is a difficult road to travel with lots of unexpected detours and roadblocks. However, if the entrepreneur is successful in moving his or her goods, the community will benefit significantly. The role of the local EDO in this case is to get out in front of the entrepreneur's truck and clear away obstacles, point out potholes, and find new routes whenever there is a detour. In other words, as with expansion and retention of existing businesses, the role of the local EDO in promoting entrepreneurship can be summarized in one word: *facilitation.*

Local EDOs can facilitate entrepreneurship and the resulting business startups by: 1) connecting entrepreneurs with the technical assistance they need to transform an idea into a business, 2) connecting entrepreneurs with lending institutions and venture capital firms that are open to providing financing for business startups, and 3) creating opportunities for entrepreneurs to interact with other entrepreneurs, professionals who provide business startup assistance, financiers, and other potential partners that can help navigate the stormy waters that often exist between having an idea and having a functioning business based on it.

RATIONALE FOR PROMOTING ENTREPRENEURSHIP

In the U.S., small businesses are in the vanguard when it comes to job creation, innovation, and economic diversification at the local level. Consequently, there is every reason for local EDOs to be active promoters of entrepreneurship and effective facilitators of business startups. Entrepreneurship and the business startups that can result from it contribute to enhancing the economy of a community in several important ways:

- Creating new jobs
- Helping to diversify the local economic base
- Helping prevent "brain drain" wherein the best and the brightest leave the community for better opportunities
- Enhancing the stability of the local economy since small local businesses are less likely to pick up stakes and leave the community
- Requiring less infrastructure support than larger businesses

Each of these reasons is sufficient to justify promoting entrepreneurship as a strategic goal of local EDOs. Taken together, they make it difficult for a local EDO to justify failing to adopt entrepreneurship as an economic development strategy.

ADVANTAGES OF SMALL BUSINESS STARTUPS

Most businesses that result from local entrepreneurial efforts are small businesses. Although a small business can, by definition, employ as many as 500 people, the typical small business startup employs 20 or fewer people. In fact, the trend in business startups is toward the establishment of *micro-businesses*— businesses that employ five or fewer people. Advances in technology that allow for home-based businesses and the increasing availability of startup capital from micro-lenders are enabling the growth of micro-businesses. Consequently, local EDOs should be sure to include micro-businesses as part of their program when promoting entrepreneurship and business startups.

Small businesses have several characteristics that make them especially attractive targets for economic development. For example, small businesses tend to have stronger ties to the local community than their larger counterparts. These ties, coupled with the size factor, make small businesses less likely to be targeted by recruiters from other enterprising communities. Another advantage of small businesses is that they tend to be more innovative and flexible and, when managed well, often enjoy relatively high profit margins. These characteristics make small businesses more capable of responding rapidly and effectively to changes in the business environment. In fact, small businesses that can survive the often difficult first four years of operation are usually so resilient that they help enhance the stability of the local economy.

POTENTIAL LOCAL PARTNERS IN PROMOTING ENTREPRENEURSHIP

In most communities, there are a number of organizations that either benefit from the efforts of entrepreneurs or are in the business of supporting them. These organizations are natural partners of local EDOs in promoting entrepreneurship. The key is for volunteer leaders in local EDOs to: 1) know who these potential partners are, and 2) establish positive working relationships with key personnel in these organizations. Potential partners in promoting entrepreneurship include:

- Lending institutions
- Educational institutions (technical schools, community colleges, colleges, and universities)
- Business and industry associations
- Professional associations
- Private training providers
- Attorneys who specialize in business-related law and services
- CPA firms
- Workforce development boards
- Chambers of commerce

On one hand, all of these organizations have a vested interest in supporting entrepreneurship and business startups. On the other hand, they all provide different types of support. The role local EDOs can play in partnering with these types of organizations is to be the common thread that pulls all of them together on behalf of entrepreneurs. The EDO can serve as a bridge between entrepreneurs and the various support providers that can help them.

STRATEGIES THAT PROMOTE ENTREPRENEURSHIP

In addition to serving as a bridge to organizations that can help entrepreneurs, local EDOs can help establish and maintain an environment that is supportive of entrepreneurship. Local EDOs and their volunteer leaders can apply the following types of strategies to establish and maintain an environment that promotes entrepreneurship:

- Identify the various partnership organizations that can help entrepreneurs, and build bridges to those organizations on behalf of entrepreneurs.

- Maintain a network of successful entrepreneurs who are willing to share what they have learned with others.

- Encourage local lending institutions to work with small business startups including micro-businesses.

- Work with educational institutions and training organizations to ensure that a skilled workforce is readily available to support small business startups.

- Maintain an up-to-date list of dependable suppliers that work well with small businesses and startups.

- Maintain positive working relationships with key decision makers in research laboratories so that entrepreneurs are aware of new technologies that might have commercial applications.

These strategies will help establish and maintain an environment in which entrepreneurship can flourish. Economic development volunteers, because of their status in the community and their business experience, can play invaluable roles in carrying out these strategies on behalf of their EDO.

ORGANIZATIONS THAT HELP ENTREPRENEURS

In addition to the partner organizations that can help EDOs promote entrepreneurship, there are a number of other organizations available to help entrepreneurs that typically are not local. EDOs and their volunteer leaders should know these organizations, the types of assistance they can provide, and how to connect local entrepreneurs with them.

Small Business Development Centers (SBDCs)

Small Business Development Centers (SBDCs) are one-stop centers for assisting small businesses. There is a nationwide network of these centers. Each center provides one-on-one counseling, consulting, training, and technical assistance for entrepreneurs and small business owners. The SBDCs are funded by the U.S. Small Business Administration (SBA). They also receive state and, in some cases, local funding.

The SBA is a federal government agency that operates under the authority of the Small Business Act of 1953. The purpose of the SBA is to strengthen the nation's economy by: 1) assisting small businesses, 2) protecting the interests of small businesses, and 3) helping small businesses recover during times of natural and economic disasters. This three-part mission makes the SBA and its SBDCs natural allies of local EDOs, entrepreneurs, and small business owners. To find the SBDC nearest your community, go the SBA's web site:

www.sba.gov

Small Business Administration (SBA) Loan Programs

In addition to funding a nationwide network of Small Business Development Centers, the Small Business Administration (SBA) also ofers a comprehensive loan program. The SBA is not actually the lending institution (except in the case of disaster relief loans). Rather, it guarantees loans that are made to small businesses through traditional lending institutions. The SBA guarantees loans that provide a longer payback period and less stringent affordability requirements than traditional commercial loans. This allows small businesses to borrow more money than they might otherwise qualify for from a traditional lending institution. The most widely-used business loans made through lending institutions and guaranteed by the SBA come under the following programs:

- *7(a) Loan Guarantee Program.* This program provides loans to help entrepreneurs with startups and existing small businesses with expansions.

- *504 Fixed Asset Financing Program.* This program is administered by a nationwide network of not-for-profit Certified Development Companies and makes loans for land purchases and construction costs.

- *MicroLoan Program.* This program makes microloans of up to $35,000 to small businesses that are too small to be considered acceptable risks by traditional lending institutions.

- *8(a) Business Development Program.* This program assists in the development of small businesses owned by socially and economically disadvantaged entrepreneurs. It is an especially important program in communities that have a concentration of federal government organizations or military bases that award contracts to private firms. One of the ways this program helps disadvantaged entrepreneurs learn to do business well enough to gain a foothold in the marketplace is by awarding them government contracts on a no-bid basis for a limited period of time.

Additional information about SBA loan programs is available at: www.sba.gov.

Small Business Incubators

Small business incubators are organizations established to enhance the survival rate of startup businesses. They can receive public or private funds or both depending on how they are established and by whom. Small business incubators are typically not-for-profit organizations that charge fees for the services provided or take an equity position in the startup firms they assist. Assisting in new business startups is the mission of incubators.

The types of services typically offered by small business incubators include: 1) office space and other physical facilities, 2) management training and coaching, 3) assistance with developing business plans, 4) administrative support, 5) technical support, 6) business networking, 7) intellectual property counseling, and 8) funding assistance.

Because of their purpose and the types of services they provide, small business incubators are natural allies of local EDOs. In fact, some incubators are operated by local EDOs. Others may be found on the campuses of colleges and universities. Still others are stand-alone organizations operated as consulting services. To find the small business incubator nearest to your community, contact the National Business Incubator Association at:

www.nbia.org.

Service Core of Retired Executives (SCORE)

The Service Core of Retired Executives (SCORE) is an organization dedicated to helping entrepreneurs and small business owners succeed. Its main function is to match entrepreneurs and small business owners who need help with retired business executives who can provide help. This function makes SCORE a natural ally of local EDOs. SCORE is a national not-for-profit organization with more than 10,000 volunteers; all of whom are available to help entrepreneurs and small business owners solve the many problems they can face with starting up, growing, financing, and managing a small business. One of SCORE's most popular services is "Ask SCORE for Business Advice." This is an on-line service that allows entrepreneurs and small business owners to receive free, confidential business advice and counseling by email. SCORE may be contacted at the following web address:

www.score.org

Minority Business Development Agency (MBDA)

The Minority Business Development Agency (MBDA) is an arm of the United States Department of Commerce that was established solely to support the establishment and growth of minority-owned businesses. This mission makes the MBDA a natural ally of local EDOs. Business development services of the MBDA include the following: 1) beginner's essentials (new business startup checklist, building your company brand, networking for success, assessing your readiness for entrepreneurship, and entrepreneurial traits), 2) preparing a business plan, 3) e-commerce, 4) technology, 5) risk management, 6) strategic planning, 7) employee issues, and 8) marketing. The MBDA can be contacted at the following web address:

www.mbda.gov

AL DONALDSON ENTREPRENEURSHIP INSTITUTE

At the beginning of this chapter, potential partners for local EDOs in promoting entrepreneurship and business startups were listed. One category of partners consisted of colleges in or near the EDO's service area. This section profiles an innovative entrepreneurship program developed and operated by Okaloosa-Walton College (OWC) in northwest Florida. The Economic Development Councils of both Okaloosa and Walton County partner with OWC in using the Al Donaldson Entrepreneurship Institute to promote new business startups in their service areas.

The Institute was founded by a team of OWC personnel which includes Dr. James R. Richburg—President of OWC, Dr. David Goetsch—Vice-President of OWC, Jim Chitwood—OWC's Executive Director for Resource Development, and retired business executive and community leader, Al Donaldson. Mr. Donaldson provided the original funding for the Institute with a substantial cash gift to OWC. The College, in turn, provided the facility for the Institute at its campus in South Walton County. The Institute is the centerpiece of that campus.

Services Provided by the Al Donaldson Institute for Entrepreneurship

The Institute provides a variety of services to promote entrepreneurship and new business startups in northwest Florida. Prominent among these are seminars, workshops, consulting, counseling, advising, networking, and referrals. The centerpiece of the Institute's various services is its periodic "Entrepreneur's Boot Camp." Entrepreneur's Boot Camp, as the title implies, is an intense program that lasts one week. During the week, aspiring entrepreneurs are provided intensive hands-on training, counseling, and specialized assistance in the following critical areas:

- Deciding if your idea has merit
- Developing a business plan
- Organization
- Licenses and permits
- Insurance
- Location and leasing
- Accounting and cash flow
- Financing your business
- Marketing
- Computers
- E-commerce

As a volunteer leader in your local EDO, the question to ask is: What does our organization do to promote new business start-ups through entrepreneurship? If your EDO has already adopted entrepreneurship as an economic development strategy, the information in this chapter will help you play a positive role in the implementation of this strategy. If your EDO has not yet adopted entrepreneurship as a strategy, this chapter will help you play a leadership role in helping it do so.

Chapter Ten

▦

WORKFORCE DEVELOPMENT

A community's workforce can be its best economic development asset or its worst liability. As a volunteer leader of a local EDO, it is important for you to understand the role workforce will play in the economic development of your community. This chapter provides the basic workforce-related information that volunteer leaders should know about the role of workforce in economic development.

WORKFORCE FACTORS

From an economic development perspective, there are four important factors relating to your community's workforce:

- Availability

▪ Quality

▪ Affordability

▪ Union or non-union

Each of these factors will be important to the prospects your EDO recruits. You need to understand how these factors figure into the thinking of companies making location or expansion decisions.

Availability

Prospects will want to know that your community has a workforce of sufficient size to meet their human resource needs. Ideally, your community will be able to provide readily available, qualified applicants for all positions the prospect will want to fill. One of the ironies of economic development is that the more successful the EDO is in creating jobs, the more difficult the process becomes because a low unemployment rate in a community can mean that a workforce is not readily available to fill the new jobs created. Prospects will want to avoid being forced into wage wars with other local employers when trying to recruit and maintain a workforce.

Quality

One of the by-products of globalization is that the quality of employee performance must improve continually in order for an organization to just stay in the race. In order to be competitive, businesses that compete in the global arena need highly-skilled employees with strong math and science skills. The majority of new jobs created in the U.S. are either technical or managerial; both of which are education intensive. Unfortunately, high school graduates in the U.S.—as a group—perform poorly in math and science when compared with their counterparts in other industrialized nations.

An additional workforce problem you need to be aware of is a declining work ethic among 18 to 30 year olds in the U.S. Business journals and books are replete with studies and cases documenting a decline in the work ethic among people in this age cohort; a critical age group for businesses hiring new employees. This decline in the work ethic has created a situation in which businesses in the U.S. are hiring new employees who have been described as people who want a job, but don't want to work. These complacent employees are pitted against their counterparts in emerging industrialized nations such as China, Indonesia, and Korea; people who have been described as being "PHDs"—employees who are poor, hungry, and driven.

The circumstances just described mean that local EDOs must forge strong partnerships with local education providers. As a volunteer leader in your community's EDO, you need to be comfortable interacting with local education officials to ensure that math, science, and work ethic are given an appropriate level of attention. Some EDOs take a pro-active approach to forging relationships with educational leaders by giving school superintendents, college presidents, and university presidents ex-officio seats on their boards. This approach ensures continual interaction between business and education leaders and is one I recommend.

Affordability

An affordable workforce is one that is available at competitive wages when compared with other communities. This is one of the reasons prospects sometimes shy away from communities with low unemployment rates. If a prospect is forced to meet its workforce needs by drawing employees away from existing employers, it will simply set off a bidding war that, over time, can cause wages to spiral upward to unaffordable levels. An exception to this situation is when a high-wage employer chooses to locate in an area with low unemployment because most of the existing jobs in the community are low paying. If an "affordable wage" for a prospect is much higher than the prevailing wage rate in your community, the prospect might choose to view minimum-wage earners as potential employees. In cases such as this, the EDO is right to recruit the prospect because an appropriate goal is not just the creation of more jobs, but also of better jobs.

Unionization

A non-union workforce is almost always a plus for a community. In fact, union activity is frequently a factor in why a prospect chooses to leave one location and find another. As businesses in the U.S. struggle to compete in the global arena, a unionized workforce can introduce factors that make it even more difficult than usual for an organization to hold down the cost of doing business. As a volunteer leader of your local EDO, you need to be prepared to answer very pointed questions about union activity; questions that are sure to be posed by prospects or their representatives.

LOCAL WORKFORCE DEVELOPMENT BOARDS

Most communities in the U.S. have access to a local workforce development board. Workforce development boards grew out of the federal Workforce investment Act of 1998—federal legislation enacted to help improve workforce preparation at the local level. Local workforce boards consist of representatives from the following types of organizations and agencies:

- Private-sector businesses (a majority of the members of these boards)
- Education providers (K-12, community college, and university)
- Community-based organizations
- Economic development organizations
- Locally appointed officials and community leaders

Workforce boards receive federal funding that can be used at the discretion of the board—within federal guidelines—to provide training and development opportunities for youth, dislocated workers, and adults. As a member of a local EDO board, you need to be familiar with how workforce boards can promote better workforce development. In addition, you should make sure that the EDO is a key player on the workforce board and that the needs of local businesses in the area of workforce development are known to the workforce board.

POTENTIAL EDO/EDUCATION PARTNERSHIPS

Because education is so important to economic development, local EDOs and educational institutions are natural partners. Consequently, as a volunteer leader of your EDO, you will want to make sure that it establishes and maintains positive working relationships with educational institutions and other community-based organizations that provide workforce training. Potential education partners include the following:

- Public and private technical schools
- Community colleges
- Colleges and universities
- Business, industry, and trade associations
- Small business development centers
- Churches and other local organizations that provide "English as a Second Language" training

An excellent way to promote partnerships with organizations such as these is to establish permanent ex-officio positions on the EDO's board for the most important of them (e.g school superintendents, college presidents, and university presidents). Another way is for members of the EDO's board to serve on the boards and advisory committees of these institutions. Partnerships are built largely on relationships. Consequently, one of the ways you can help your EDO is to establish and maintain positive working relationships with local education officials.

WORKFORCE DEVELOPMENT STRATEGIES

In addition to creating ex-officio positions for education leaders on the EDO's board and serving on the boards and advisory committees of educational institutions, some EDOs choose to take an even more pro-active approach to workforce development. This section provides examples of workforce development strategies that are partnerships between a local EDO and other organizations involved in some aspect of workforce development.

The Quality institute

The Quality institute (TQI) is a partnership of the Okaloosa Economic Development Council (EDC) and Okaloosa-Walton College (OWC). TQI provides two types of training for business and industry firms in Okaloosa County, Florida. The first type consists of customized workshops offered on or off-site for specific firms. Only personnel from the firm requesting the training may participate. In this way, the training can be customized to deal with specific issues of concern or specific areas of weakness that need to be strengthened in the business in question.

The second type of training provided by TQI consists of generic seminars that have broad appeal and are open to all members of the EDC as well as non-members. Members receive a per-participant discount on the admission fee. Customized and generic training are provided by TQI in the following areas:

- Leadership
- Management
- Supervision
- Customer service
- Strategic planning
- Teamwork
- Change management
- Quality management (a variety of individual topics)
- Six sigma
- Lean manufacturing
- Managing the "me-generation"—turning "me-players" into "team players"
- Establishing and maintaining a high-performance corporate culture
- Managing the unmotivated—transforming "slackers" into producers

- Enhancing the work ethic of employees
- Various technical topics

The partnership between the EDC and OWC works like this: 1) the EDC receives requests for help from member firms (for customized training) or the EDC develops an on-line brochure to advertise an upcoming generic seminar; 2) the College provides the instructor and, in the case of generic seminars, the facility; 3) the EDC registers the students and handles the logistics of checking in; and 4) the College and the EDC split the remaining revenue after deducting the cost of the instructor and any other expenses.

Leadership Okaloosa

Leadership Okaloosa is a partnership of four chambers of commerce in northwest Florida and Okaloosa-Walton College. The chamber partners are the Crestview, Destin, Fort Walton Beach, and Niceville-Valparaiso Chambers of Commerce. The mission of Leadership Okaloosa is to help "rising stars" from the private, public, and not-for-profit sectors develop the skills needed to be effective leaders in their organizations as well as in the local community. Participants meet once a month for a year. Eight of the meetings take place in OWC's Corporate Training Center and four are field trips. One field trips is to the Florida Legislature in Tallahassee and one is to nearby Eglin Air Force Base—the economic engine of Okaloosa County. The other two field trips are selected by participants from a frequently updated menu of possibilities.

Classroom sessions begin with a structured networking activity so that participants can develop positive working relationships with their fellow leadership students. Networking is followed by various leadership development activities which include lectures, discussions, simulations, role playing, and guest speakers. Each successive leadership class is responsible for selecting and carrying out a class project. In order to complete the project, participants must learn to develop a strategic plan, work together as a team to implement the plan, and lead small groups in carrying out various aspects of the plan.

As a local employer and volunteer leader in your EDO, you are in a unique position to interact with local education officials in an informed way. If your organization has workforce needs that are difficult to meet or are going unmet, the same is likely to be true of other organizations including prospects and start-ups. By maintaining positive working relationships with local education officials, you can help correct or, at least mitigate, such situations.

GLOSSARY

Affordable housing. A common term in contemporary economic development circles. It refers to housing that costs no more than 30% of household income. It becomes a factor in economic development when the personnel organizations need to hire cannot afford to live in the community where they will work.

Basic industry. Organizations in this category are the principal target when recruiting new businesses to a community. Basic industry organizations export their products and services thereby bringing new money into a community from outside of the community. For example, manufacturers are typically base industry firms.

Brownfield. An abandoned or under-utilized site that is contaminated or thought to be. Such sites, depending on their contamination status, sometimes become industrial sites.

Business climate. The attitudes of government, local citizens, other businesses, and the local workforce toward business. Prospects look for a positive business climate and are typically very sensitive in perceiving less than positive attitudes.

Business Recruitment. A fundamental activity of most local EDOs, it involves attempting to attract businesses from outside the community and convince them to locate locally.

Business Retention. A fundamental activity of most local EDOs, it involves systematic efforts to meet the needs of existing business so effectively that they remain in the community. Most retention efforts are aimed at helping existing businesses: 1) increase sales, 2) decrease the cost of doing business, and 3) improve the business climate.

Capacity building. Developing a community's ability to effectively conduct an economic development program. Typical activities include efforts to improve the business climate, establishing an effective local EDO, and marshalling the commuity's resources to support the EDO's efforts.

CDBG (Community Development Block Grant). Federal block grants for communities of 50,000 or more residents provided under the auspices of Title 1 of the "Housing and Community Development Act of 1974." CDBGs are typically used to improve the health and welfare of the community by improving economically blighted areas.

CDCs. Not-for-profit organizations that receive federal funds to assist in the provision of affordable housing. Some of the funds received by CDCs can be used for economic development.

Clawbacks. The name given to penalties built into economic development incentive contracts. These penalties require businesses to either repay or forego payment of selected incentives if they fail to perform according to contractual obligations.

Development authority. An agency—typically non-governmental—established with the authority to issue bonds, levy special taxes, and enact regulatory requirements.

Easement. The right to use another's property for a specified purpose (e.g. an easement granted to an electric utility company to erect power poles and lines across a portion of someone's property).

Economic base. The foundation of a community's economy. It is composed primarily of basic industries (those that make products locally and export them bringing money into the community from the outside) and service industries that simply circulate money within a community.

Econometric modeling. A qualitative analysis method used to predict the effect of economic events or activities. For example, econometric modeling can be used to determine the overall impact of recruiting a new business to the community or the effect of losing a business.

Economy of scale. A phenomenon in which costs are reduced as amounts are increased. For example, in manufacturing the cost per part produced is less as the number of parts increases. In a service business, the larger the order of a given supply, the less each individual item in the order will cost. These are only two ways that the concept of economy of scale applies. There are many others.

Enterprise zone. Designated areas that are singled out for special incentives. An enterprise zone is established as an economic development strategy to attract private investment. For example, in order to redevelop a blighted downtown area a community might seek to have it designated an enterprise zone. Businesses that agree to locate within the zone receive various types of incentives such as tax mitigation.

Flexible-use space. A business or industrial facility that can be used for a variety of different applications such as manufacturing, distribution, office, etc.

Gap financing. Financing that fills in the "gap" between what an economic development project can support and the cost of development.

Geographic information system (GIS). A concept enabled by high-powered computer hardware and software that integrate social, geographic, economic, and demographic information and presents it in a useful form. For example, a GIS system can produce a map that contains much more than just the typical geographic information. It might also contain demographic, social, and economic information relating to the area in question. Further, as to geographic information, the system can produce a drawing or map that shows every feature that exists in the area on, under, and above the land. Those local EDOs that use GIS have a great advantage in being able to give prospects so much relevant information in such a concise format.

Impact fees. Fees charged by government agencies to cover the costs of the various ways a new development "impacts" the local infrastructure. For example, impact fees might be charged to cover the cost of connecting a new facility to water and sewer or installing curbing and gutters to accommodate parking/ingress/egress.

Incentives. Various economic development strategies that decrease the cost of doing business. Incentives are awarded to encourage businesses to expand, start-up, or relocate to the community providing the incentives.

Industrial development bonds. Financing—usually tax exempt—made available under specific conditions to pay for acquisitions, construction, expansion, and/or the purchase of new equipment.

Industrial park. A specified area set aside and zoned for industrial use. Industrial parks typically have very specific covenants governing property use. Similar concepts are technology parks, commerce parks, and research parks.

Industry cluster. Concentrations in one geographical region of similar and often complementary businesses. For example, a region might have an industry cluster composed of aerospace manufacturers and suppliers. Often local EDOs will base their recruiting strategies on targeting a given industry cluster.

Localization economies. A phenomenon in which the cost of business is reduced as the number of businesses of a given type that locate near each other increases. Perhaps the best example of this is the fast food industry wherein several competing fast-food restaurants will locate at the same interstate highway exchange; a practice that reduces marketing costs for all of them.

Microenterprise. A very small business employing five or fewer personnel and often only one. A plumber with a set of tools, a truck, telephone number, and a website would be classified as a microenterprise.

Often microenterprises are operated out of the owner's home.

Multiplier effect. Additional income for local communities generated by dollars that flow into the community from the outside. For example, when a manufacturing firms brings new dollars into a community from the outside, the value of these dollars is multiplied because they will then circulate within the community.

Penturb. A small metropolitan area located outside of but in proximity to a major metropolitan area. A penturb is farther away from the major metropolitan area than a suburb and it is independent of the major area.

Revolving loan fund. A fund of public and private dollars set aside for loans to businesses that is "revolved" in that as loans from the fund (with interest) are paid, the money is used to make another and the process repeats itself.

Seed capital. Funding provided to a business to help it get started (i.e. to "seed' it). Seed capital is typically private money provided by a person who takes an equity position in the business in question.

Smart growth. The most efficient and effective use of a community's assets to accomplish economic growth.

Special assessment districts. Designated areas established by a taxing authority. Businesses within these districts are levied additional taxes beyond those paid by businesses outside of the district. For example, businesses located within a special assessment district on the coast might be assessed additional taxes to cover the cost of beach restoration as storms periodically erode beach frontage.

Sustainable development. Development that does not tend to erode the natural resources and assets of a community. Sustainable development typically consists of projects that are environmentally sound and that tend to enhance the overall quality of life in the community.

Tax abatement. Reduction in the amount of taxes paid under specific conditions and for a specified period of time.

Venture capital. Money that is invested—usually at significant risk—in businesses perceived to have high potential. Venture capital is typically reserved for projects that have the potential for very high returns over a relatively short period of time.

Zoning. Categorizing geographic areas according to their acceptable use (e.g. commercial, agricultural, residential, manufacturing, etc.).

Printed in the United States
By Bookmasters